Creating Future Memory

Success is a biological fact. Success is achieved based on memory. Your memory, particularly how you remember accords with your success, which is a function of biology and not a function of your mind. Memory is the key to accomplishment because *memory is the entirety of your life experience*. What you remember and how you remember determines all life. Everything is memory. Everything is based on how you remember, and as you live in your moments, every moment becomes an instant memory, which in turn contributes to your success. You can shape that memory.

Why is memory important?

How you remember your moments determines how you feel, and how you feel determines your success. How you feel determines what you accomplish. Feelings also are a matter of biology and not a matter of the mind. What you feel is essentially a chemical reality within your body, and every feeling has a molecular structure which constitutes chemical arrangements within your body called hormones. These *hormones and their movements within your body determine whether or not you are successful.* That's right. As a matter of fact, hormones are the sole determinate of your success and even your failures. It is your body, not your mind that is the sole entity that pushes you towards accomplishment or away from accomplishment.

This workbook is very unique in nature, because I will be sharing with you biological facts that contribute to your success and winning. This highly unique approach is entirely different from other practices as it concerns coaching you towards your exact determinations. I will start by charting out the reality of how success really works. In this, you might have to relinquish other understandings of what success is.

Here's the point. *You are biologically geared for success and you are biologically composed for accomplishment.* This is the first understanding that you must have which is an absolute truth. Let's take a closer look:

What you decide to remember and how you decide to remember is vital towards the health of your body. Here, there are two forms of memory to consider. Past memory, and then future memory.

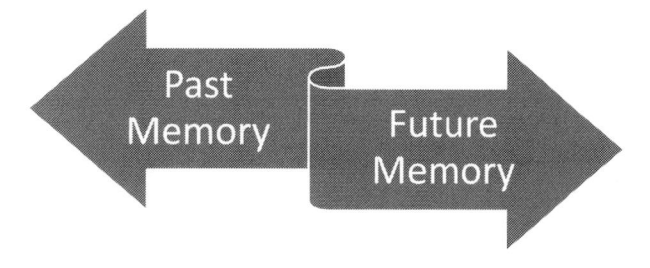

⬅ Past Memory | Future Memory ➡

Your Hormones Can Read and Respond to Both Past Memory and Future Memory

As you choose between past or future memory; yes, *"future memory" is a thing*, you must note that future memory is a memory that is constructed and developed by you. Once done, your body treats your future memory in the exact same manner as it does past memory. As a matter of fact, the way to treat unwanted or buried past regressions is to create sufficient future memory wherein the energy of your body can retain a new focus. Memory is memory, and your mind can't differentiate between past and future memory. Whatever memory you choose to focus on, your body will compose and complete the following "biological event.

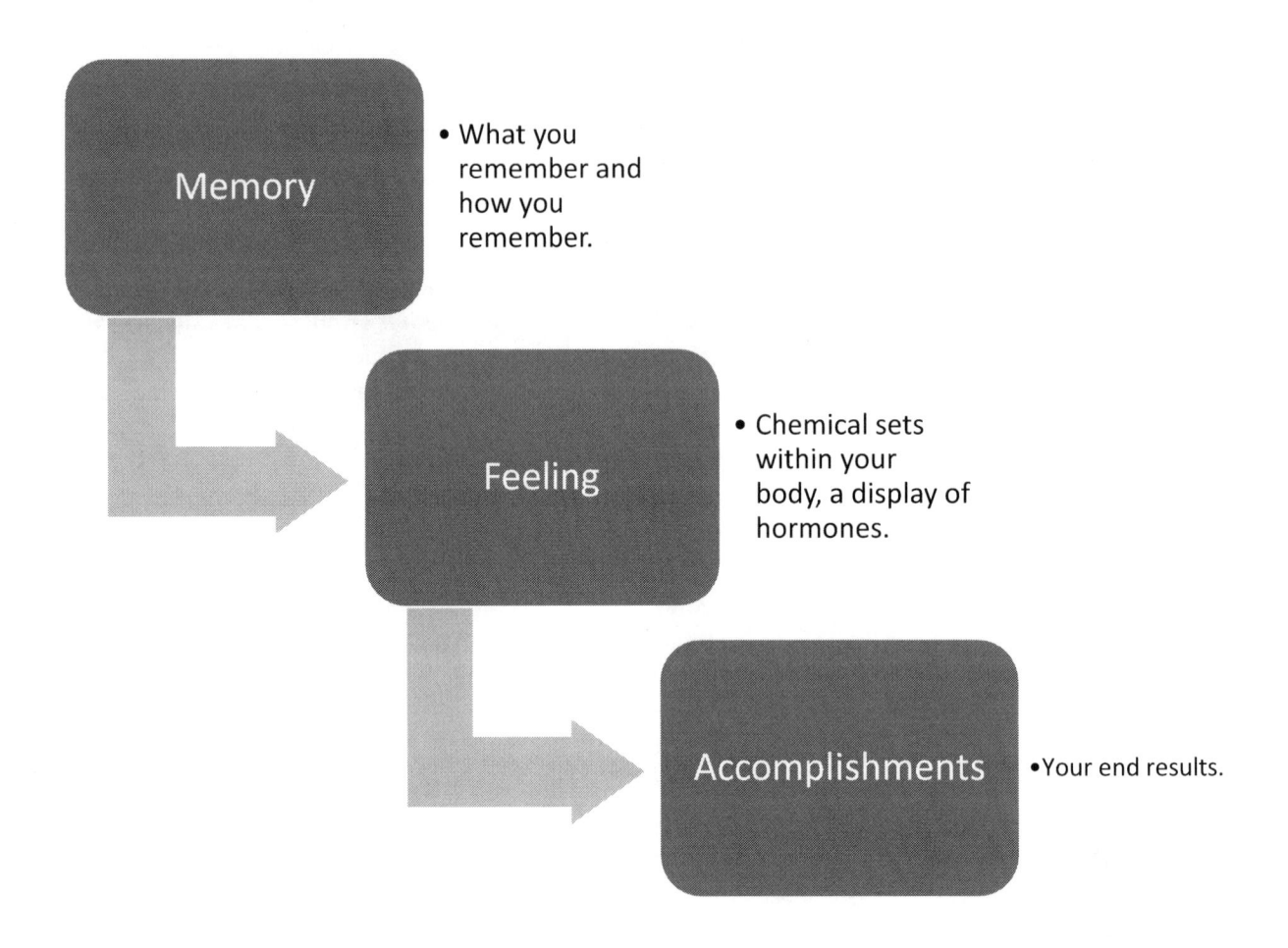

- **Memory**
  - What you remember and how you remember.

- **Feeling**
  - Chemical sets within your body, a display of hormones.

- **Accomplishments**
  - Your end results.

This is a biological event!

I'm going to give you the basics here, but will later on give you more exacting details. What is extremely important is that you become intimately familiar with what I just shared with you. In essence, **you control your accomplishments by how you decide to remember and what you decide to remember**, and then subsequently, how you feel. When you are dissatisfied with the results in your life, it is because you have a progression of memory recalls that is formulating those results.

You actually control what you remember. If you don't know this, it then becomes impossible to control your memory, which in turn, it then becomes impossible to determine how you feel and subsequently control what you accomplish. To know this information is paramount. In order for this workbook to work for you, you must establish within your consciousness this exact reality. I will give you the details of the functionality of this process that guarantees your success. Yes I said it. **What you want to accomplish is guaranteed by nature. This is a biological fact. Biology as it concerns the human genome is about accomplishment.**

Let me explain. You are a biological reality amongst many other biological realities. When it comes to the plant and animal kingdom, you are the crowning point of all biological reality. As a matter of fact, **all other biological realities are created to invest into who you are and what you want**. Everything outside of your physiological presence is designed as a contribution towards your own personal determinations. This is a simple fact, yet it is an extreme fact. The entirety of the Universe functions to serve you and what you determine to be. In order to understand these facts, you must understand your physiological makeup. Once again, you are designed for success. You are designed to be successful.

The Question of Failure

If human beings are physiologically designed for success, why do so many people fail? That's actually an easy answer. **People fail because they don't remember to win**. What do I mean by this? Everyone knows how to win. Everyone knows how to reach their desired goals. Everyone knows how to accomplish their designed destiny. Everyone knows exactly how to be successful. The problem is this, not everyone remembers this part of themselves.

There are distinct distractions to ultimate memory. This inevitably is the truth. Nothing is random and everything is determined by something or someone. There is no such thing as good or bad luck, only what one determines and subsequently remembers. I'll give you an example that you can identify with.

When you reach a point where things or something doesn't work, for the most part, you commonly express the fact that you knew that this was to happen. You dated that man or that woman, and when things didn't work out, you get this express feeling that you already knew that it wasn't going to work. The time when you lost quite a bit of money, and at that exact moment it comes to mind that whatever action you took that caused you to lose the money, you knew it was the wrong move. It's like when something doesn't work, at the point when it doesn't work, you knew that it wasn't going to work in the beginning. Right?

It's "awww man, I knew it"! "I knew I shouldn't have called that girl or that man. I knew I shouldn't have gone here or there. I know I shouldn't have said this or that. I knew I shouldn't have given money!"

Why is that?

The Peril of Options

You always know the truth, but for the most part, you immediately become distracted to absolute truth and thusly move down a non-optimal path. When that path reaches a dead end, you then become acutely aware of the fact that you should not have taken that path. You always know. **You must be careful of distractions once you have determined your path to success**. Distractions are interruptions to the truth. The truth is, you know exactly how to win, but something distracts you from the path of your distinct determination. I call these distractions...**OPTIONS**.

Distractions are simply options to what you really want. You simply just do something else besides what you know to do in order to accomplish your goals. People do it all the time. They say one thing and then do another, and then cry about what's wrong. They never acknowledge the fact that they have completely lied to themselves about their behavior pattern that leads them astray and away from what they really want. Unbelievable!

People have desires, and when they don't accomplish their desires, they are unable to admit that their choices lead them to an undesirable state. They blame it on life, God, other people, the weather, good luck or bad luck, karma, and everything else. They do not stop long enough to realize that they inevitably adopted an "*option*" outside of what they wanted and subsequently moved in a different direction. This is because what they remember is controlling their behavior patterns. Memory is this powerful.

Memory 101 – How you Decide!

Memory is the source of all future behavior. Every event is expressed as a moment, and every moment immediately becomes a memory. Memory is essentially the "stuff" of life. The entirity of life, "except for fleeting present moments" is memory. ***Moments don't count, how you remember your moments is what counts***. Memory determines how the chemical sets or how the hormones move and are arranged within your body. ***It is these blueprints of hormonal activity that become the source of your behavior patterns. Hormones are the source of all your activity and not what you decide towards an activity***.

You never decide what to do, you only decide how you feel. You might think that you decide your behavior and activities, but in reality, ***your behaviors and activities only launch themselves off of the reality structures of the hormones within your body.*** You might think you decide what actions you take; but no, this is a misplacement of decision-making. You never decide your actions. You never decide your behavior. Your actions are a subsequent determination of hormonal behavior, hormonal placement, and the hormonal array within your body. ***Your actions are always mirrored from how you feel***. This is when some people make a decision for certain things to happen, and then they never take action towards it. Why? They simply don't feel like it. *Your hormonal activity is your truth*.

What I will show you is how not to make decisions on what actions to take in order to accomplish what you want, but to remove decision-making from the point of deciding what to do, to deciding what you remember. Once this is set, your actions then become autonomic. This is a biological reality and I don't want you to take this lightly. *I am going to show you how to get exactly what you want by not deciding how you're going to get it, but by deciding what you remember according to the future, which in turn guarantees what you want*. So let's look at this chart again, but I will add in your behavior patterns and the actions that you take.

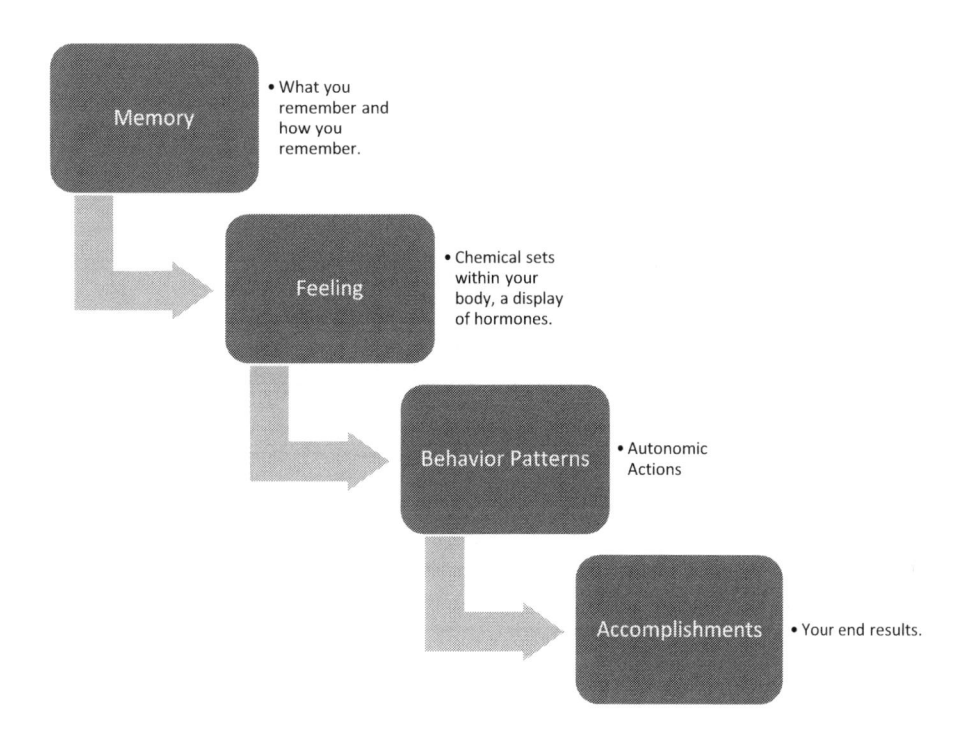

```
Memory — What you remember and how you remember.
   ↓
Feeling — Chemical sets within your body, a display of hormones.
   ↓
Behavior Patterns — Autonomic Actions
   ↓
Accomplishments — Your end results.
```

Please digest this chain reaction. This chain reaction is a biological function. Why do I say that?

You will be surprised at how much of what you want is already accomplished. *Your body and its biological functions directly contribute to your desires*. Your body is built for that. This is an awareness that I'm bringing to the table. And with this being the truth, you must succincly know that the decision-making capacity was placed in the wrong compartment of your reality. Inevitably, *you're not supposed to decide what actions to take, you must use the energy of decision-making to decide what you remember and how you remember*. This is why past memory in so many cases is such a strong determinant on how a person behaves, and subsequently the success or non-success of that individual.

Yes. ***Stop deciding what to do, and start deciding what you remember***. This is vital and of extreme importance. Decision-making is misplaced when you are deciding what to do. When you decide what to remember then you are on point, positively and even negetively.

The Addiction Reality

Addiction is what exists between what you feel and how you behave. The surprising fact is that ***your body is designed to be addicted***. Addiction is at the base of any and all accomplishment. How driven are you? What are you intricately tied to? What you are intricately tied to is what you will accomplish. Let's look at some standard addictions and learn from the subsequent behavior patterns.

Alcohol addiction.

Opioid addiction.

Sugar addiction.

Nicotine addiction.

Caffeine addiction.

Now let's look at a few addictions that are considered to be nonstandard or nontypical addictions.

Addiction to unhealthy relationships and people.

Addiction to a religion or a cult.

Addiction to a job.

Addiction to video games or social media trolling.

Addiction to poverty cycles. Essentially, addiction to being poor.

There is even an addiction to failure. This is where the elusive practice of self-sabotage becomes heightened.

Addictions are attachments that control behavior. The defining point of addiction is that the results are seemingly immediate and seems to be something that is effectively controlled by the individual with the addiction. Addiction is a form of control, generally because the outcomes are essentially guaranteed. Meaning, you know the end of the story, and that becomes a point of comfort in terms of relying on the addiction. The high is guaranteed, the paycheck is guaranteed, the abuse is guaranteed, even the dissappointment is guaranteed. The pain is guaranteed. You know what's coming. **Addiction provides assurance**.

The reason why the body does such a great job at addiction, which most people consider to be a dysfunction, is simply that ***addiction is not a dysfunction***. Addiction is not a dysfunction and the stigma must be removed from the reliance on addiction. ***Addiction must be repurposed so the body can accomplish your desires. This is an orginal evolutionary design specific to the human genome***. As a matter of fact, those who are considered to be prone to addiction actually live in an advanced state.

The secret is this, ***all behavior patterns are launched off of addiction and not decisions***. Contrary to popular belief, you do not make decisions to take action. You are predisposed to addictive behavior. All behavior is launched off of the chemical realities within your body, which are specially placed hormones within your body that dictate your behavior.

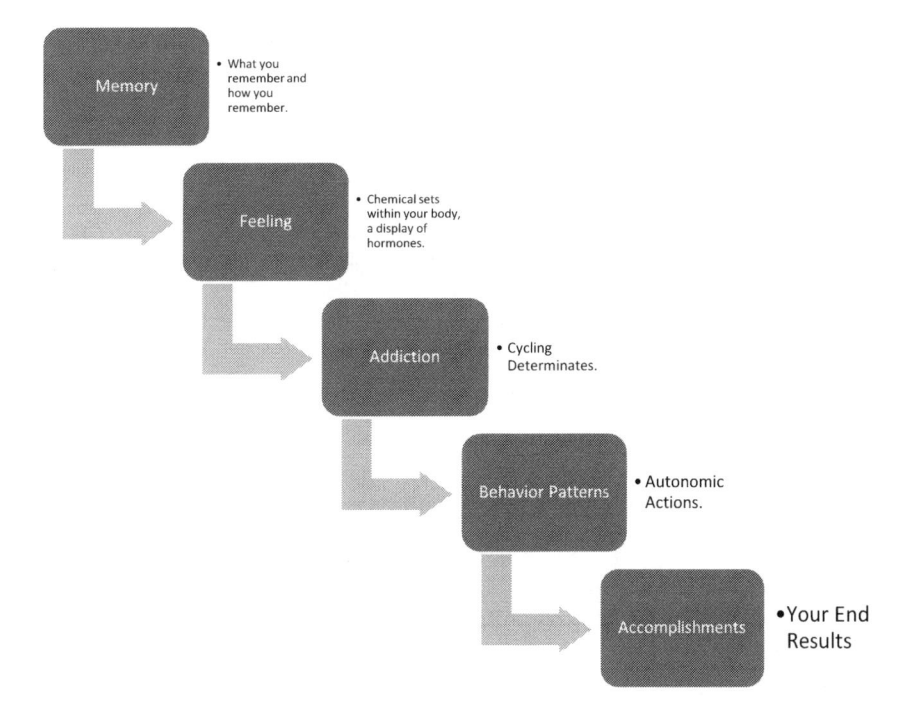

- Memory
  - What you remember and how you remember.
- Feeling
  - Chemical sets within your body, a display of hormones.
- Addiction
  - Cycling Determinates.
- Behavior Patterns
  - Autonomic Actions.
- Accomplishments
  - Your End Results

Everyone on the planet is an addict, not just those hooked on crack cocaine, heroin, cigarettes, pain pills, alcohol etc. What scientists need to learn as they come up with a way to resolve the "problem" of addiction, is to realize and then remember that addiction isn't a problem at all. Memory is where the problem really starts. ***When you control the memory, you control the addiction, because addiction is a natural state and not a dysfunctional state.***

Since the body is designed for your success, which I will prove from a biological standpoint, then addiction is designed for what you're trying to achieve and not for illicit substances. ***Substances and other forms of addiction are simply a replacement for achievement***. As a matter of fact, substance abuse is a form of achievement. This is why I stated that those who are addicted to substances are more advanced because of the appropriate lineup of how to determine behavior. Those with nonstandard addictions, for the most part, don't even know that they're addicted. This is extremely dangerous. Many who find themselves unable to accomplish what they want are simply addicted to the "options" to their dreams. They can be addicted to going in many unprofitable directions and the suffering that comes with it.

Not only does nonproductive forms of addiction need to be changed, but one must form and create new forms of addiction to replace addictions that don't work and in addition, don't give the desired results. Those with nontraditional addictions have their addictions masked. Meaning, they don't even know that there needs to be a change because their addictions are not stigmatized. Therefore there's no reason to move from an unsuccessful behavior pattern to a newer productive behavior pattern. Essentially, they are hooked on what doesn't work, but are entirely clueless that the habitual patterns are blocking their true desires.

Notice, a drug addict does not let anything stand between them and their drug. Even dignity will have to go out the window in order to accomplish the substance. This is truly an advanced state of being and accomplishment. ***If you learn how to be addicted to your dream, then you will truly learn not to let anything stand between you and what you want***. This is the formula for extreme success. A drug addict is successful and practices their success every day. How much time do you spend on your dream?

When you are not addicted to your dream or destiny, you will be addicted to something that is less fulfilling, because your body is designed to be addicted.

I will provide you with strategies that will assist in removing patterns that distract you away from or interrupts what you want to accomplish. But a good portion of this book has to be geared towards sharing with you new information that provides the foundation for this new technology of accomplishment. Within this, you must learn some new things about your body.

First, **your body is the true home of your subconscious**. Any psychologist would tell you that it is your subconscious patterns that rule your end results. When you try to accomplish one thing, and another thing happens, this is traced back to the subconscious or what psychologists call subconscious beliefs or subconscious memories. Your body and the movements of hormones are a mirror of expressed behavior patterns and events outside your body, and the hormonal movement within your body is the subconscious. This provides a map of what is considered to be the mental movements of the mind, but in actuality, it is the physiological movements of the hormones that is the mind housed in the body.

Let me be clear. **When you are feeling something, you are not thinking**. When you feel something, the next natural response is a behavior. When a parent chastises a child for doing something seemingly stupid, they will always reverberate this statement, "What were you thinking!!!". In actuality they weren't thinking at all, they did what they felt like doing, not what they thought they should do. Thinking had already gone out the window. Primarily, kids don't think when they get into something, they just get into it. They weren't thinking, they just did it. They felt it. The feeling was dominate.

This is another example of the successful inner-workings of the body. **We do too much thinking versus moving**. Again, thinking should be applied to your memory and not your behavior. That's why when people try to change, they can't do it. They spend too much time considering options versus specifically considering what they're trying to accomplish. With this, most people spend their time being all over the place versus moving in one direction. This is because they are answering fear.

The Question of Fear

First, **there is no such thing as fear**. Fear is a designed reality used to describe the function of what is really a hormone secretion from the adrenal gland. This design reality is not a true reality. It is entirely man-made. Again, there is no such thing as fear. There only exist the reality of a hormonal presence that causes you to feel a certain way. But what is this feeling really telling you?

Now were getting into the biological reality of what causes you to be great. What you sense as fear is not fear at all. From your adrenal gland, there is a hormone that is secreted called epinephrine, more recognized as adrenaline. When this is released from the adrenal gland, adrinaline moves through the bloodstream in response to an outer event. Psychologists call this the "fight or flight" response. What this is, is actually just a heightened sense of awareness. It makes your abililty to focus more keen.

In actuality, this "fight or flight" response is a result of a presentation in front of you that will bring up questions. In standard cases, this is when something is presented in front of you and you must then respond. For example, a huge grizzly bear surprises you as it stands 9 feet tall on its hind legs and there seems to be an imminent attack on your well-being. Adrenaline rushes through your body, and you call this fear. So at that time you must determine this, do you run or do you attack the bear. Fight or flight.

Let me share with you another example. The same bear raises up with all the ferocity that can be mustered up, along with the roar that can intimidate the mightiest of lions. The bear is easily 1500 pounds, but faces a woman that is a mere 125 pounds. Let's say, that as the bear stands there with all of its potential power to annihilate the little woman, but the woman's tiny six month old baby is laying at the feet of the bear. The woman rushes the bear, jumps up before the bear could make a move, and begins gouging out the bear's eyes. The bear, now in severe shock and pain, drops down and runs away.

Did that woman experience fear? The answer is no. She had the same adrenaline rush, but expereinced a different behavioral response because the situation warranted it. Make sense? **Adrenaline is a response, not a fear**. There is no such thing as fear. Only the presence of adrenaline or epinephrine. It's a chemical. That's it. But in the case of the little 125 pound woman, the same adrenaline was used to educate the woman as to how to attack the bear. How did she know what to do?

It was the education outlined in the adrenaline. Like a little kid who has to write lines on a piece of paper as a punishment from their parent or teacher, I would say, "write the following statement 100 times until you actually get it into your system".

An education is outlined in every adrenal response by the adrenal gland.

When you experience what you consider to be fear, the question comes up, what should I do or what should I not do? How will I handle this? Then there's a sense of paralysis because you end up in the space of not knowing what to do. What you normally consider as being fear can be paralyzing in nature. But at the same time, what you consider as being fear is not fear at all. **With adrenaline, you are being presented with the education of how to get past what's in front of you. Adrenaline is an opportunity to know something different, new, and what's next**. This is what the woman used to attack the bear without question. Her baby laying at the feet of a ferocious bear removed all questions and other options, and only presented the option of attacking the bear.

Essentially, the state of "fight or flight" is present at all of your decisions. The state of "fight or flight" is present at every decision that you make or have to make, but it is there to provide you with an education, not just a two-way decision. **There is the presence of epinephrine or adrenaline at every decision you make**. This simply means, by the time you're ready to make a decision, the education towards that decision is already in place. This is how intelligent your body is. In essence, **by the time you dream a dream and decide towards that dream, your body is fully educated as to how to accomplish that dream**. But a lot of times we mistake the presence of this chemical as fear and then we back off.

The adrenal glands are two glands that sit at the top of each of your kidneys. Each gland has three layers. The magic of alchemy takes place every day through this particular function of your adrenal glands. As cholesterol passes through these three cellular layers of the adrenal gland, the cholesterol is reduced into a different substances at each stage.

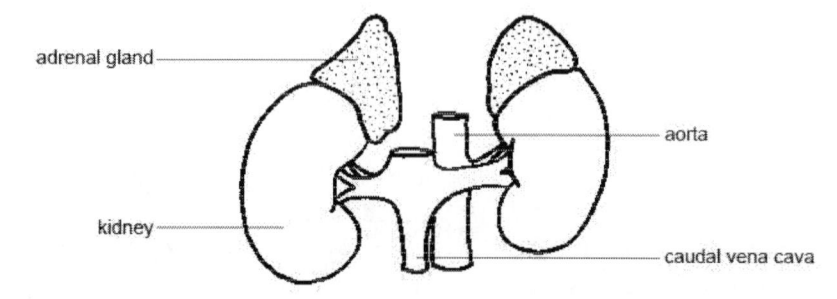

Adrenal capsule

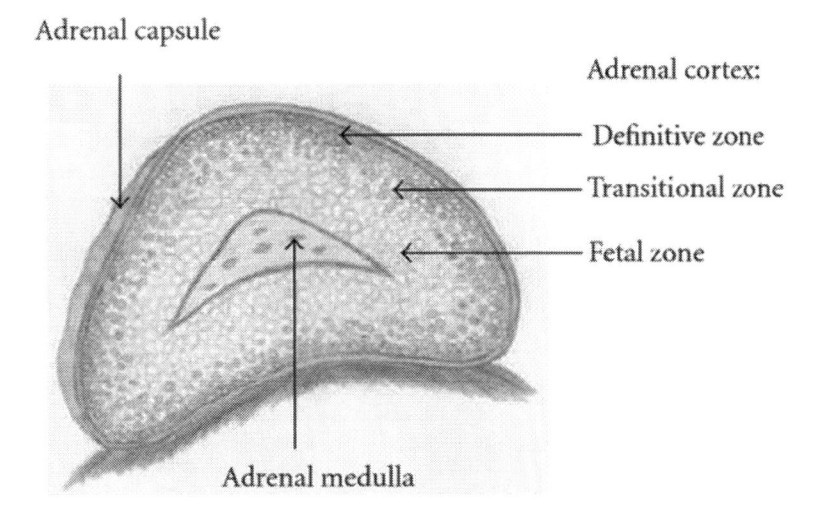

Adrenal cortex:
- Definitive zone
- Transitional zone
- Fetal zone

Adrenal medulla

As cholesterol passes through these zones, the cholesterol reduces into a different state within each layer. The molecules tranfrom from cholesterol, to salt, then to sugar. ***This sugar in your adrenal gland is a function of memory***. The sugar at this point is crystalising what you want in life. The sugar at this stage is called glucocorticoids, a steriod hormone that eventually impacts your adrinaline flow. After the "sugar stage" comes a "definition" or defining stage, which extends from the memory function of the glucocorticoids. Specifically, testosterone, estrogen and others, which are defining hormoes follow the formation of this sugar. Adrenaline or epinephrine is a response to this biological layout. In early biological systems, this process was formulated strictly to determine the male and female sex, but in the human body these "definitions" extend to so much more, including your dreams and your designed destiny. This whole process now becomes a contribution to your success.

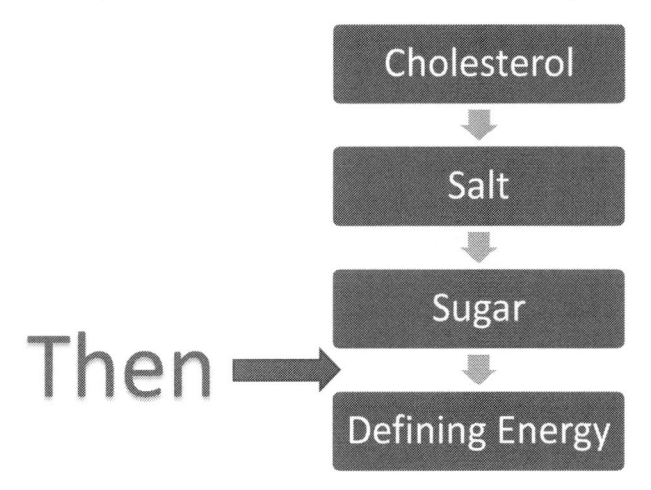

Then ➡
- Cholesterol
- Salt
- Sugar
- Defining Energy

This is a natural conversion process that takes place within your body every day. This conversion process in your body is a response to a mental blueprint based on your perception. ***I must be clear, events do not influence the adrenal gland. It is how you perceive those same events that impact your adrenal gland***. Contrary to popular belief, the question of ***cholesterol in the body is less tied to your diet, but more significantly tied to how you perceive things***. It is your perception that forms into a memory.

The Gift of Perception, Conception, Exception & Reception

Your perception also impacts the hypothalamus located in your brain, which in turn impacts your pituitary gland, then in turn impacts the adrenal gland and its respective responses. Most psychologists or psychiatrists study this system primarily in terms of how stress works and the impact of stress upon the body. But **the adrenal system is designed not just for stress response, which is a minute function of the entire system, but it is mostly designed to respond to your outlook and perception**. There is a designated biological response to what you want in life, and it is exclusivly based on how you perceive your dream in relationship to the circumstances and events around you.

Meaning this; how well and how intact does what you want and your destiny remain as a point of focus when things around you shift? What do you see when others can't see? To what extent do you hold on to the desire of what you want when there is no evidence to support what you see? *Your adrenal gland honors consistency. Your body goes to work, not only to remind you of the direction that you're going in, but it goes to work to educate you as to exactly what to do to accomplish what you want - EDUCATION*. This is the purpose of your adrenal gland. You have a built-in system that's designed to keep you on track if it is properly used.

Again, there is no such thing as fear, only the provision of information that helps you to accomplish what's next. Your personal biological system is designed for what's next. It is not designed to sit still or to go backwards. When you make a determination to sit still, settle, or go backwards; your body will let you know through dysfunction and sickness. **Disease is never a happenstance, it is a result of turning away from a specific designed destiny**. Your body supports forward progression, and anytime you think otherwise, it will begin to shut down. This initially starts as adrenal fatigue and will subsequently affect every other organ in your body. To avoid this, I will deal with the following four stages of development as an exercise for you.

- A. Perception
- B. Conception
- C. Exception
- D. Reception

Perception

I want to note here that perception is where you use your thinking power and decision-making power. You do not use your thinking power and decision-making power to determine an action. Mmmmmmm. You use your thoughts to determine your perception. You use your thoughts to formulate optimal memory.

What do I do? Is not the question. What I choose to see, is the answer!

Thoughts = Perception
Thoughts ≠ Actions

The resulting processes built within your body will then determine your actions. This is why goalsetting is useless. Setting parameters of time to accomplish something is useless for most people. This is why people make a list, and then nothing happens.

Your perception must be shaped and your body will then respond accordingly, starting with your hypothalamus, extending to your pituitary gland, then through the impact that it has on your adrenal gland by promoting the processing of your cholesterol into sugar. This ***sugar then becomes a force of nature***. Glucocorticoids. Notice the following:

Alcohol is sugar.

Of course, table sugar is sugar.

Heroine is sugar.

Cocaine is sugar.

Highly fascinating, isn't it?

Glucocorticoids are responsible for what scientists call "flashbulb memory". Have you ever had a "flashback"? This is when something that was experienced as a negative event in your past that was sparked by a similar present event. The memory of the horror that you experienced in the past becomes a highly intensified phsycological event which adds on to the event that you are currently experiencing. Here, the past event contributes to your current reality. Your current reality is then intensified, whatever that reality might be.

This is what happens when your body is not trained to remember correctly. Bad thoughts becomes more readily available than good thoughts. Why is this?

Well I'm glad you asked.

The key here, is future memory. The function of flashbulb memory or flashback memory was a primal function of the human experience. The advanced function of this same system is to ***take in future memory***, which will have the same impact on your body as past memory if you install the future memory to replace the past memory. What am I saying here?

You are physiologically designed to dream and to create greater future realities. When you don't, your past realities will be enhanced. Your future should have a greater impact on your body more so than your past reality. ***It is your future that should shape your perception and not your past.***

Before going to an exercise for developing perceptions that's controlled by future realities that you create, I want to share this short example from my friend Dr. Milton Howard Jr. from his book The Anatomy of Significance – The Answer to Matter and Meaning. This section is called "The Anatomy of Memory".

The Anatomy of Memory

The tree has fallen in the forest. The tree has fallen in the forest across a road, blocking the road. The tree has fallen in the forest, blocking the road, but has landed on a car. The tree has fallen in the forest, blocking the road, but has landed on a car with a family in it. The tree has fallen in the forest, blocking the road, but has landed on a car with a family in it, and the family was hurt. The tree has fallen in the forest, blocking the road, but has landed on a car with a family in it, and the family was hurt, and there were emergency vehicles everywhere. The tree has fallen in the forest, blocking the road, but has landed on a car with a family in it and the family was hurt, and there were emergency vehicles everywhere while it was pouring down rain.

Several people witnessed this event. The local news station was on the scene interviewing several witnesses asking them, "What happened?". Here are their answers:

Witness #1, a forester said, a tree fell.

Witness #2, a busy businessman said, the road was blocked, and I was late for work.

Witness #3, a curious child said, I saw a whole bunch of lights flashing. Pretty…

Witness #4, a concerned citizen said, a whole family was injured in an accident.

Witness #5, a clueless bystander said, I was stuck in the rain.

Witness #6, a driver in the next car said, a tree just missed hitting my car.

Witness #7, a car enthusiast said, a Mercedes Benz was crushed by a tree, Oh my God.

Witness #8,   a doctor said, there were multiple contusions and lacerations, but the family is ok.

Witness #9,   a nervous person said, I saw the accident, my heart stopped, I started sweating etc.

Witness #10, an aspiring actress said, look Ma, I'm on TV.

There is one event, 10 different takeaways. What happened? What is reality? You have hundreds of thousands of ways to process a single event! You are never locked into what you decide to remember.

Life is a response to how and what you process in the mind that then becomes memory, starting with the formation of an electrical impulse and water called neurons. Now in addition, there are chemicals in your body that respond to the construct of these neurons in the brain, and your body itself becomes a "responsive enforced memory" that mirror these neurons. Scientists view these chemicals or hormones that are experienced via its movements as emotions.

Your body is simply a composition of chemical movements and secretions. They move quickly through the brain via the neurons and then the body chemically as you process events within the mind. Even though this all happens within nanoseconds, every event that is witnessed by you can be processed to benefit you. You can bypass the initial reactions to any undesired event and create new ones. Even if the event is well in the past, and especially events that haven't occurred yet.

This is the initial construct of the mind. This is the mind as it responds to events. This is the mind as it responds to the environment. Your first point of control in all of this, is what's done in that nanosecond of time between an event, then the impact of that event upon your senses. It is here that ***you must train your mind how to process events so that every event is processed to benefit you***. Yes, ***every event that is witnessed by you can be processed to benefit you***. Meaning, good or bad, negative or positive, no matter the type event, you can create new neurons based on how you decide to take in and process events. Remember, the event is not the reality; the processing of the event is the reality. Life is what you decide to carry within you as memory.

Remember, the event is not the reality; the processing of the event is the reality.

Note this carefully, "bypassing initial reactions to events and creating new ones". Again, ***your thinking cannot be applied to the actions*** you will take in response to an event, but more correctly ***applied to how you perceive or see the event***, which in turn determines your personal experience. Even past memory can be reexperienced as you go back and look at it differently. This is the power of perception.

Let's take a close look at what happens… hear what happens… feel what happens.

This is what happens in the following simultaniously:

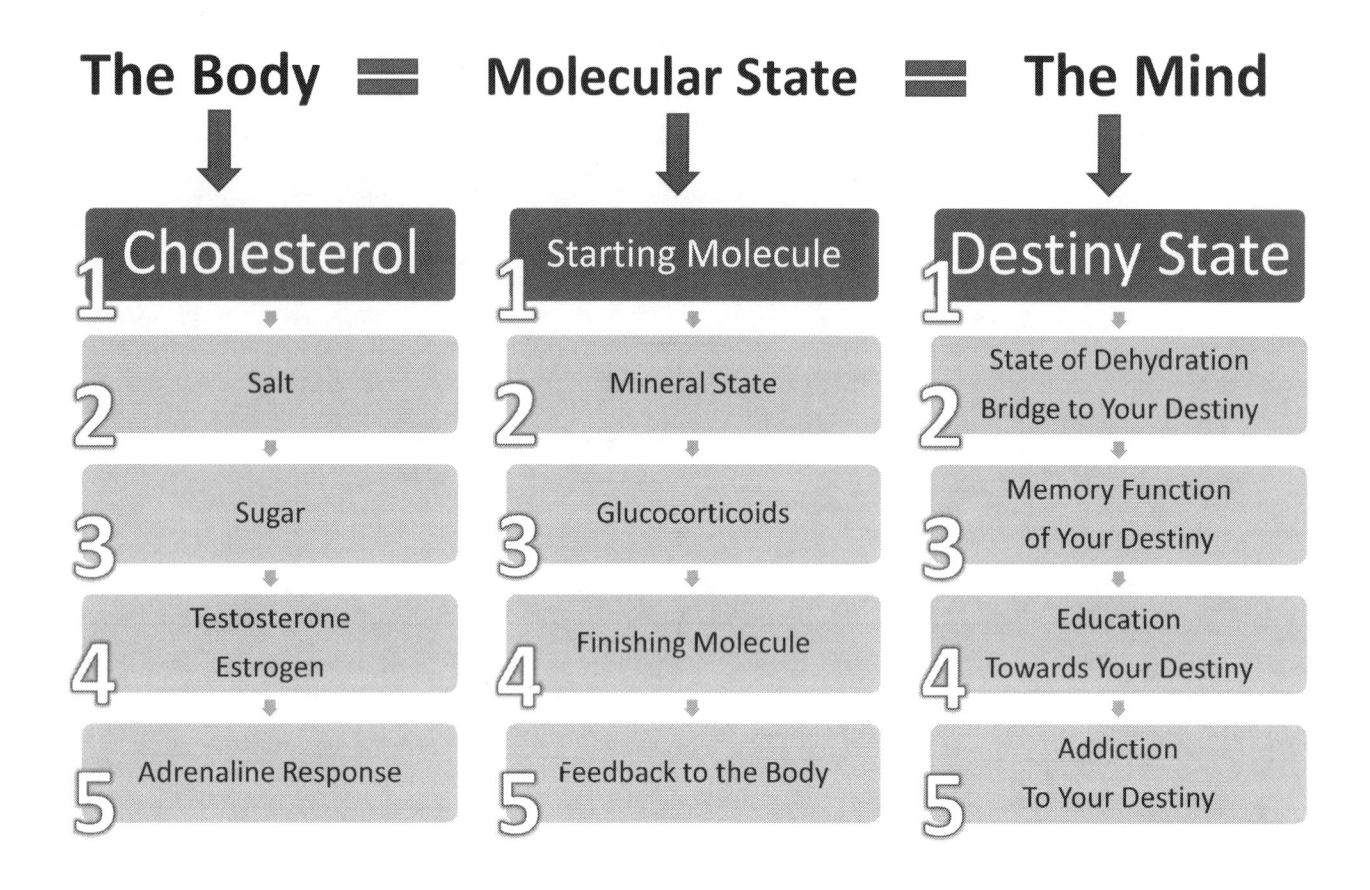

The Body	Molecular State	The Mind
1. Cholesterol	1. Starting Molecule	1. Destiny State
2. Salt	2. Mineral State	2. State of Dehydration / Bridge to Your Destiny
3. Sugar	3. Glucocorticoids	3. Memory Function of Your Destiny
4. Testosterone / Estrogen	4. Finishing Molecule	4. Education Towards Your Destiny
5. Adrenaline Response	5. Feedback to the Body	5. Addiction To Your Destiny

Located in your body, this is a process that takes place witin your adrenal gland. Cholesterol converts into salt. Then the salt coverts into sugar. The sugar then converts into estrogen and testosterone. Once this conversion is completed, adrenaline then spreads through the body depositing in the cells the education of the actions needed to accomplish your end game.

It is what you decide to remember that influences this whole process. It is then that this process, once completed, it forces action.

You do not think then act. You think to determine memory; what you remember and how you remember. This impacts your cholesterol, which inevitably impacts your adrenaline. Then you act.

Based on your perception, the cholesterol in your body travels in two different directions. You see here the impact on the adrenal gland. But cholesterol also impacts the neurons in your brain.

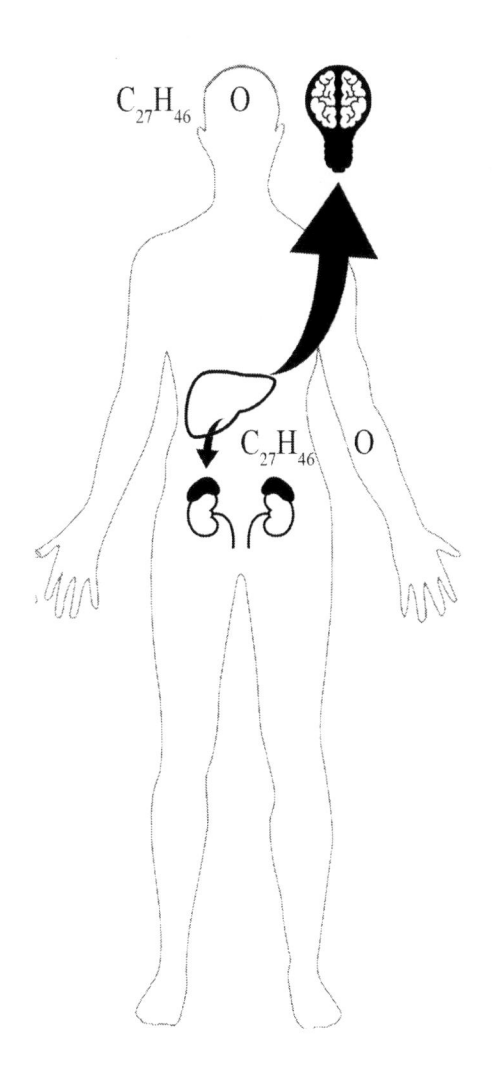

Cholesterol flowing to your brain to become your idea in the form of neurons.

Cholesterol flowing into the Adrenal Gland to become the memory of your idea.

Here you see the cholesterol that's created in the liver as it moves to the adrenal gland, and it also moves towards the brain. ***The same cholesterol that makes the salt and sugar in your adrenal gland, is the same cholesterol that creates the neurons in your brain***. Why am I sharing this with you? Every *"thing"* starts with an idea. Your cholesteral biophysically responds to your idea. You must have an idea to optimize the functioning of this process within your body. Your liver needs an idea, a new creation, or what's next to produce cholesterol that is consistent with the succcess you desire.

It must be clearly understood that ***your perception is what creates memory*** and not an event. ***Your body responds to your perception and not the circumstances that surround you***. To shape your perception, you first must be clear about what you want in life.

Here are the four areas you must be clear about:

1. Passion and Purpose
2. Lifestyle
3. Money
4. Relationships

These four must be established in order for it to impact your perception. It must become the totality of your thinking. As you experience an event, it is these four items that you would use to determine the meaning of that event. **All thinking is launched off of first, your passion and your purpose. Second, the lifestyle you want. Third, the money you want. And last, the relationships that you would like to experience.**

It's like a basketball player shooting free throws. There's some unique basketball players who rarely miss their free throws. It doesn't matter how much the audience yells and screams at them. It doesn't matter the negative comments that they get from the opposing audiences. Their focus is so intense, that they barely know that the crowd is even there. Why? I want you to take note of this; when it comes to free throws and a shooter being that good, that player is not making the shot based off of skill, they are making the shot based off of memory. This is why they shoot 300 free throws a day. They are building the memory of making the shot, and when it comes to crunch time, they are simply doing what they remember. Making the shot is no longer a skill but a memory.

In the same light, when you know your passion and purpose so well, it doesn't matter the circumstances around you, you only respond to the future based on your memory and not your circumstances. But you must create the memory in order for it to work. You will be surprised at the number of people who have no idea as to what they want in life. Without an idea, a dream, a destiny or knowing what you want, the body cannot function optimally because **your body is designed to respond to your future reality and not your present tragedies**. If you do not have a designed future reality, your present tragedies, whether they're great are subtle, they will work through your body by default.

Perception

What is your passion and your purpose?

Your answers cannot be general, like: helping people, making money, or living my dream life. Your answers have to be specific and purposeful. The energetic response of your body does not know how to read general answers. I inserted some examples of this section for you to model. If you have to take the information and just insert your desires, that's fine.

High Impact Statements : Use Extreme Language

Why are you here? What's your reason for living?

_____
_____
_____
_____
_____

What is it that you would love to do? Write it in detail.

_____
_____
_____
_____
_____

If money wasn't a concern, what would you would be doing?

_____
_____
_____
_____
_____

What are your talents and gifts?

_____
_____
_____

Combine these four answers and compile them into your passion and purpose similar to the following examples.

This is my life's personal design that comes as a result of my vision based on what is already inside of me. Every statement is who I Am, and by choice I choose to live me, my greatest self.

SAMPLE 1

PASSION & PURPOSE

I AM AN IDENTITY COACH

I am providing services that move persons from a state of paralysis to focused movement that lead to accurate and intended results. I am a specialist who unwraps a person towards who they already through specific discovery techniques and strategies. I am bringing out their presence which states their future.

I AM SHARING MY STORY WITH EXTEME IMPACT AND RESULTS TO THE LISTENER & READER

I am delivering my story with precision, causing those who receive my story to identify their own troubles as starting points to their greatest selves. I am speaking my story from the worlds greatest stages, I am delivering my story in all major book stores worldwide, and I am sharing my story on major television networks on cable and on demand.

I AM AN ACCOMPLISHED & AWARD-WINNING AUTHOR

I am experiencing my literary works on the New York Times best-seller list. I am presenting my books on morning shows such as Good Morning America with Robin Roberts and Gale King on CBS. I am also sharing strategies within my book with Oprah Winfrey on Super Soul Sunday. My books are selling on a million-based platinum level many times over. I am recognized amongst the greatest personal development authors of all time including; Tony Robbins, Jack Canfield, and Napoleon Hill.

I AM A WORLD-RENOWNED SPEAKER

I am mentored by the #1 speaker in the world, Les Brown. I am traveling to some of the world's greatest destinations sharing my story. I am experiencing audiences of 5000 plus people per event. I am hosting events and seminars that are constantly selling out. I share the stage with Oprah at her "Your Best Life" events. I am being used by Oprah and many other thought leaders as their Identity Mapping specialist.

I AM A CELEBERITY COACH

I am bringing Identity Mapping to celebrity and athletic clients, eliminating the need for such Institutions as Scientology and Kabala practices. I am providing Identity Mapping that sets their future and settles their present.

Be sure to use as much as you can the words "I Am". You cannot use the following phrases:

"I want to be."

"I will be."

"I would love to do this are that."

You must use the phrasing "I Am". This keeps everything in the present as you write out your future. This becomes your truth and will more accurately have your body to naturally respond to it. Here's the second sample that you can you use.

SAMPLE 2

PASSION & PURPOSE

I AM MAKING MY KIDS HAPPY
I am providing my kids a tremendous sense of security wherein they are free to be themselves and take risks to be their greatest selves.

I AM MAKING MY KIDS FEEL LOVED
I am presenting myself to them as a present mom deeply in every aspect of their lives.

I AM LIVING MY HIGHEST ADDICTION
I am addicted to my purpose in life. I am waking up every day to the greatest part of who I am.

I AM AN EVENT SPECIALIST
I am creating and hosting events wherein I am making thousands of dollars per event. I am the best event coordinator, bring my skills of planning, decorating, arranging, and chef skills to the table. I am also creating and hosting the best parties that causes the client to experience memorable moments that is well worth the money that they spend.

I AM A PERSONAL CARE SPECIALIST
I am great at making people feel good. I am impacting lives by bringing personal care skills to individuals looking for rejuvenation. I am the best at any personal care techniques, including massage, hair, and nail care.

Make a specific heading starting with "I Am" and then do your description with "I Am" starting each sentence. Use the four questions that I asked to formulate these personal affirmations. Make at least 4 to 5 headings and then be detailed in your description. You are literally painting a picture of who you are. This is important.

I AM _____

_____
_____
_____
_____
_____
_____
_____
_____
_____
_____

I AM _____

_____
_____
_____
_____
_____
_____
_____
_____
_____
_____

I AM _____

_____
_____
_____
_____
_____

I AM_____

I AM_____

You must remember that you are impacting your cholesterol, which goes both to your brain to form neurons and to your adrenal gland to form sugar. When you give yourself purpose, you give your cholesterol purpose. Think of cholesterol as a paintbrush. As you speak your purpose and passion, which is your personal truth, your cholesterol paints your body with this truth. **You cannot afford to not design your future.**

If you are a corporate employee and your desire is to move up in the company, you must paint the picture of where you going well before you get there. Your body in response will take care of the rest. Generally, our problem of accomplishment is that we never determine what that accomplishment looks like. Whatever it is, you must **spell it out and be absolutely clear in your description**. The body does not work correctly without a clear description.

The next thing that you must be clear on is your lifestyle. Here are some examples of how to spell out or draw a picture of your lifestyle.

SAMPLE 3

LIFESTYLE

6 BEDROOM, 7 BATHROOM HOME

I am living in a wonderful spacious home. I am walking into my greatest space which has a full chef's kitchen with a commercial grade oven. I am enjoying working in the personal spa I have in my home to care for my family, providing ultimate relaxation sessions. I am looking into the rooms that I have created for each of my kids with a space that matches their character and talent. I am enjoying an incredible pool space and outdoor kitchen which is perfect for entertaining the guest coming to my home. I am on the first floor where my husband has a personal office and we share a fully functional gym...etc. etc. etc.

TRAVEL

I am traveling with my husband and kids to some of the world's greatest destinations including: Jamaica, Hawaii, the Cayman Islands, Bora Bora, and Italy. I am flying first class with all of my family, and because I have people working for me, I am traveling often...etc. etc.

MY CAR

I am riding in my brand new 2020_____. The uniqueness of the color is making my _____ a standout. I am dropping my kids off at school and they step out of our car with great pride. I am also driving a _____ because of its unique style and comfort...etc. etc.

MY HEALTH

I am wearing the size clothes I want. I am eating the best foods that contribute to life. I am exercising daily as a part of the maintenance of my extreme vitality.

Again you are taking the time to be very specific about your lifestyle. Here also, you would need to spell the things out using "I Am" at the start of your phrases. Here's a second example that you can use.

SAMPLE 4

LIFESTYLE

4 BEDROOM, 3 BATHROOM HOME
I am living in a wonderful spacious home. I am walking into my greatest space which has a full chef's kitchen with a commercial grade oven. I am enjoying working in the personal spa I have in my home to care for people looking for the ultimate relaxation session. I am looking into the rooms that I have created for each of my kids with a space that matched their character and talent. I am enjoying an incredible pool space and outdoor kitchen which is perfect for entertaining the guest coming to my home.

TRAVEL
I am traveling with my kids to some of the world's greatest destinations including: Jamaica, Hawaii, the Cayman Islands, Bora Bora, and Italy. I am flying first class with all my kids, and because I have people working for me, I am traveling often.

MY CAR
I am riding in my brand new 2020 purple MKX. The uniqueness of the color is making my SUV a standout. I am dropping my kids off at school and they step out of our car with great pride. I am also driving a Ford Edge because of its unique style and comfort.

You must know your lifestyle in order for it to become a memory. You cannot afford to leave any of this to happenstance. You must be the definer. You must be the designer. You must be the determinant. Write out your lifestyle.

My Home

_____
_____
_____
_____
_____
_____
_____
_____
_____

Where do I Travel?

_____
_____
_____
_____
_____
_____
_____
_____
_____

My Transportation

_____
_____
_____
_____
_____
_____
_____
_____
_____
_____

Be sure not to leave anything out. Be very specific in your description. **Your description leads to your destiny**. Be sure to know that your body will accurately read all of this information and turn it into a chemical formation that supports where you're going. Not only does it support where you're going, you will also have the education to make it to where you want to go and to accomplish what you want to accomplish.

The next affirmations is the description of your money. As I said before, there is a good number of people who are addicted to poverty cycles. They are addicted to things not working out, When you do not become descriptive of your money, your money will always exist in a confused state. Again, this is the process of building memory. If you do not build the memory of what you want, your body has nothing to go on in order to accomplish its desires. Describe your money. Here are a couple of examples.

SAMPLE 5

INCOME & MONEY

- I am making $5 million to $7 million per event.
- I am making $75,000 plus per speech.
- I am making $500,000 per month in book sales.
- I am making $43 million per year to start.
- I have 120,000 customers paying $99 per month minimum.
- I am making $1.5 million extra a month with 5000 clients or products.
- I am always getting more jobs and clients than I expect.
- I am making an extra $8 million per year with Celebrity clients.
- I am making $43 million per year.
- I am a sought-after speaker and personal Identity Coach specialist with people ready to pay me top dollar for what I do.
- I am valued among the best in the industry personal development, identity mapping, and personal care wherein people will always pay more than I charge them.

SAMPLE 6

INCOME & MONEY

- I am making $3000.00 - $5000.00 per event
- I am making $5000 plus per party I plan
- I am making $5000 plus per month
- I am making $60,000.00 per year to start
- I have 20 personal care customers paying $200 per month minimum
- I am making $4000.00 extra a month with personal care clients
- I am always getting more jobs and clients than I expect.
- I am making an extra $48,000.00 per year with personal care clients
- I am making $108,000.00 per year
- I am a sought-after event specialist and personal care specialist with people ready to pay me top dollar for what I do.
- I am valued among the best in the industry of event planning, party planning, and personal care wherein people will always pay more than I charge them.

As you can see, I gave you a couple of different options. Especially here, you do not want to limit yourself. Fill the following out to your exact specifications.

FILL IN THE FOLLOWING

INCOME & MONEY

- I am making $_____ to $_____ per _____.
- I am making $_____ plus per speech.
- I am making $_____ per month in _____.
- I am making $_____ per year to start.
- I have _____ customers paying $_____ per month minimum.
- I am making $_____ extra a month with _____ clients or products.
- I am always getting more jobs and clients than I expect.
- I am making an extra $_____ per year doing_____.
- I am making $_____ per year.
- I am a sought-after _____ with people ready to pay me top dollar for what I do.
- I am valued among the best in the industry wherein people will always pay more than I charge them.

Push the numbers until you feel it in your body. Do not be shy about the truth that you want to show up in your life. ***Your body carries the intelligence to take a picture of what you want and begin to produce a roadmap to get there***. I will explain this a little further later. Now, let's define your relationships. There's nothing to fill out here, because I don't want to take a chance in you describing your desired relationships in the wrong way. ***Relationships are the most vital to the health and responsiveness of cholesterol movement***. So I will share with you the following that's not up for debate or discussion.

SAMPLE 7

RELATIONSHIP

- I am Viewed. People see the truth in me.
- I am Understood. People hear me.
- I am Engaged. People work with me & my ideas.
- I am Praised. People say great things to me.
- I am Believed. People agree with my greatness.
- I am Prioritized. People put me first.
- I am Enriched. People support with money.
- I am Advanced. People support with time.
- I am Rewarded. People return to me what I give.
- I am Exalted. People invest praise in me.
- I am Increased. People invest their talents in me
- I am Mirrored. People complete me.

These are 12 points of investment that everyone needs. It is your relationships that play a foundational role in your perception. What I would like for you to do so you can digest this information, is to spell out each one as I have given it to you. This way you can start taking in the feeling of what these mean. Trust me, you need all 12. Re-write the 12 above in the lines below.

1._____
_____

2._____
_____

3._____
_____

4._____
_____

5._____
_____

6._____
_____

7._____
_____

8._____
_____

9._____
_____

10._____
_____

11._____
_____

12._____
_____

This is how you create your future reality by using the four affirmational the components.

1. Passion and Purpose
2. Lifestyle
3. Money
4. Relationships

This future reality becomes memory built within your body. It then shapes your perception. What do I mean by this?

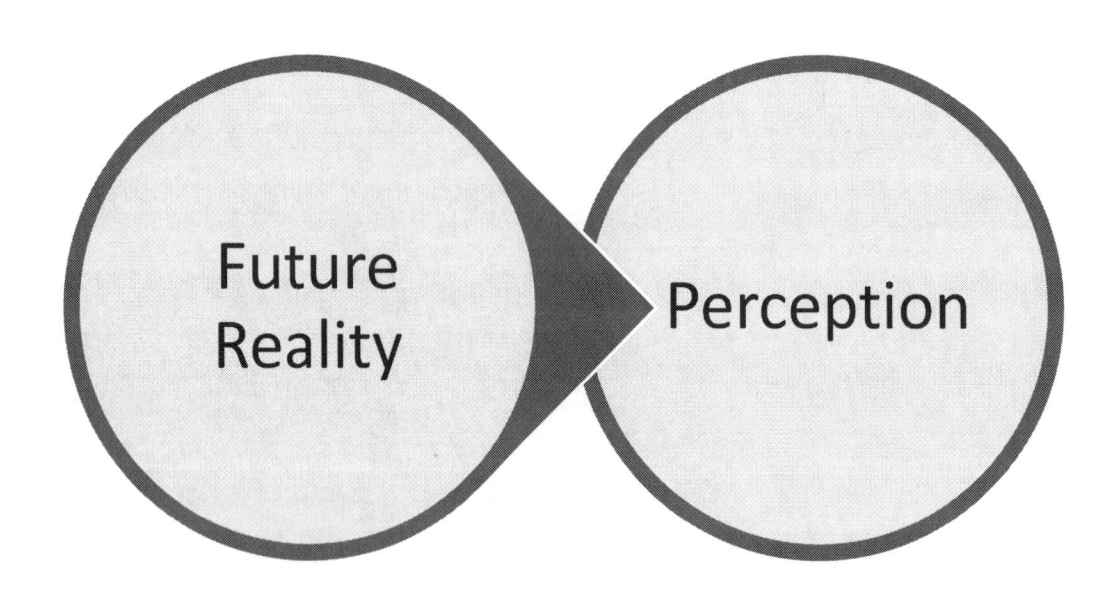

Future Reality → **Perception**

Let's revisit the question of fear, then the creation of a lie or (options to your truth). Ok, you have now created a future reality. You have designed your passion and purpose, lifestyle, money, and a roadmap to your desired relationships. This reality expresses itself as a memory in the formation of sugar in your adrenal gland. This simply means that when an event comes up that's not optimal towards your destiny, you will immediately be reminded of who you are, why you are, what you are and where you are. For the most part, this is where people get scared and create options to this truth.

But let me remind you, you are designed to consistently advance. Biology came into existence to promote your advancement. What do you see?

There is always a "Truth Beyond" your current circumstances. When you listed the four categories of affirmation and advancement which was specifically designed by you, your cholesterol mirrors this advancement and writes it into your brain by building neurons that tell the same story, and then within the adrenal gland in the form of glucocorticoids, it is also scripted there to remind you of the exact same story. When the epinephrine or adrenaline is released into your body as a result, this signifies that you are now educated as to how to accomplish your destiny. You must open yourself up to this fact.

The question is, do you follow the presentation of the "educational anxiety" towards your greatness, or do you settle into your current circumstances in order to feel safe. **Options will always be presented to you against your desired destiny, but you must not only perceive the truth beyond these options and your current circumstances, you must act on the truth of what you really want**. Otherwise, anything else that you act on accordingly will be a lie towards your own truth. An option towards your own truth.

Think about this…

Why are you advanced beyond all other existences and species? **You can take in the event, both negative and positive and assign it to your future as a positive**. This simply means that you see everything from the standpoint of your future. When something bad happens, instead of focusing on what's wrong, you take that event and use your designed perception to relate it to your future.

What's next will always seem to be too much to handle. Think about it. **Capacity and Capability**

CAPA – is the root of these two words. Cap or Capital – It's all about learning and understanding your capacity and then learning what you are capable of. This is why I am sharing with you the intricacies of your body and its biological nature, which is the nature to promote your success. **Your body has been in training for a long time just to make you successful. Your body is designed to contribute directly to your success**.

Think about these guys…

Jobs, Elon Musk, Gates, Wright brothers, Tesla, Edison (Lighting Manhattan). The risk. The men who built America. JP Morgan, Rothchild, Carnegie, JD Rockefeller, and the Walton's which were the infamous tycoons of the past.

What about the pioneers whose names are synonymous with the word pioneer? Going where no man has gone before. Think about the female pioneers of current industry like Oprah, Melinda Gates, Martha Stewart, and such.

TS Elliot puts it this way, "Only those who go too far, knows how far one can go…".

In this corporate environment, the one who knows what's next, wins. Your body is designed to hold what's next. You must learn about its capacity and capability, so I will continue to show you the wonders of your biological makeup.

There's always been a deep dive when it comes to studying the brain and its capabilities, but the secret here is that it has never been the brain that's driven the advancement of your ideas nor the cultivation of those ideas. It has always been the body and its functions. The brain is simply a transfer station and carries a small function of memory maintenance (A neurotransmitter response that mirrors into a hormonal response throughout the entirety of the body, which becomes a function of memory, which in turn parks itself in your DNA).

The key here is memory and the function of memory. Your body not only remembers the past, but your body is designed to remember the future and build future memory. What's out there? The answer is everything, even all the "new stuff". **How do you get to the new stuff? How do you innovate? You remember it.**

When options present themselves, which ultimately leads to distraction or a distance from action, you must allow the memory of your destiny to rule, much like the basketball player remembers to make a free throw. It is not a skill, it is memory. With this being said, you must practice your memory.

Practice what you remember about your future!

First, fully understand that there is past memory, but what you establish for the future becomes memory also. Within this, you must practice your future.

1. Practice Your Future
2. Enhance Your Future with the Right Relationships. (Meaning those who agree with you 100%. There is absolutely no space for hope... or you will live within a false pseudo paradigm...)

In order to practice your future, you must become extremely clear about what you want. This then becomes the foundation to how you see everything else. In every situation and circumstance, you have the opportunity to practice your future. You define the immediate things in front of you from the standpoint of your future. **Every immediate event is a gift towards your future**, good or bad. It all depends on how you perceive it. Your body is a listening and recording device, everything that you do and everything that you perceive funnels through your bloodstream into this very biological process.

If you are not addicted to your destiny, you will be addicted to what doesn't ultimately serve you.

All of your addictions settle here, where the story of your designed destiny processes.

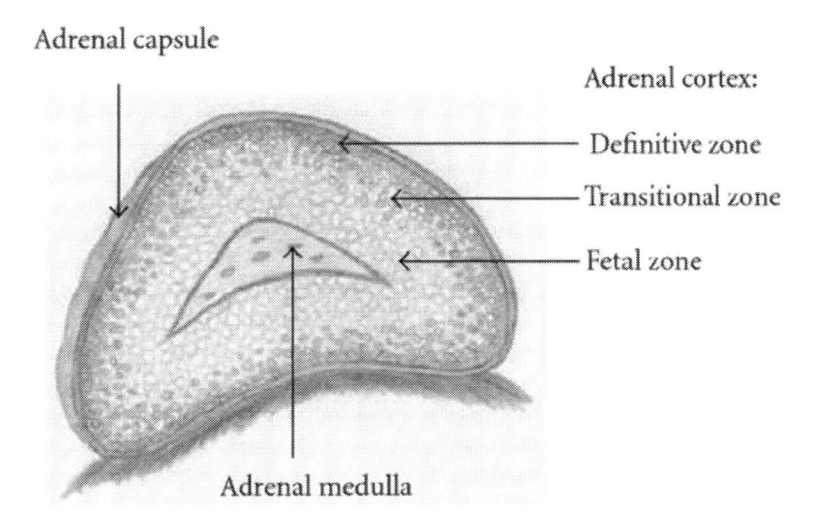

Adrenal capsule

Adrenal cortex:
- Definitive zone
- Transitional zone
- Fetal zone

Adrenal medulla

1. How You See Things
2. Your Every Action

⬇

Adrenal Gland

⬇ ⬇ ⬇

Cholesterol	Starting Molecule	Destiny State
Salt	Mineral State	State of Dehydration Bridge to Your Destiny
Sugar	Glucocorticoids	Memory Function of Your Destiny
Testosterone Estrogen	Finishing Molecule	Education Towards Your Destiny
Adrenaline Response	Feedback to the Body	Addiction To Your Destiny

This is why it is vital to control your perception and your actions well before an event takes place. **When you control your perception and your actions before an event takes place, then you control the event and the event does not control you**. It does not matter what happens to you, it can be reshaped into the way you want to see it, especially as it concerns your future. Just like the basketball player is in full control of his free throw shot well before the audience was there to scream at him in order to cause a distraction.

To do this, you must first take your passion and purpose and practice that any way you can.

Example:

1. A person has an extreme passion for baking. Every time they ride past a bakeshop or a bakery, they can clearly see themselves working at that bakery.
2. Another person has an extreme passion for baking. Every time they ride past a bakeshop or bakery, they can clearly see themselves owning that bakery.
3. Another person has an extreme passion for baking. Every time they ride past a bakeshop or bakery, they can clearly see themselves owning a chain of bakeries all over the country.
4. Another person has an extreme passion for baking. Every time they ride past a bakeshop or a bakery, they can clearly see themselves owning a chain of bakeries all over the country and having their own television show baking.

All four has a specific passion for baking, but four different perceptions of how that plays out. You must realize that your perception is what's invested into your adrenal system. If you only believe you can get a job at a bakery, that's what you will remember. If you believe you can own a bakery, that's what you will remember. If you believe you could own a series of bakeries throughout the country, that's what you will remember. If you believe that you are a superstar baker and is baking daily on TV, along with owning a series of bakeries, that's what you will remember.

There might be some who have a passion for baking and drive by that same bakery or bakeshop and say, I could never do that. That's what they will remember. And their subsequent actions will reflect what they decide to remember.

True memory is a function of the adrenal gland as cholesterol flows into the adrenal gland to become the memory of what you perceive, therefore what you practice.

1. How You See Things
2. Your Every Action

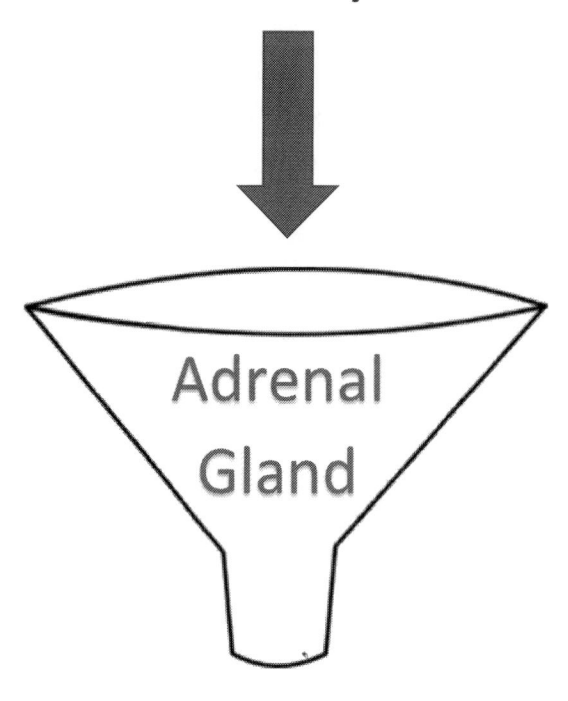

⬇

Adrenal Gland

Adrenal capsule

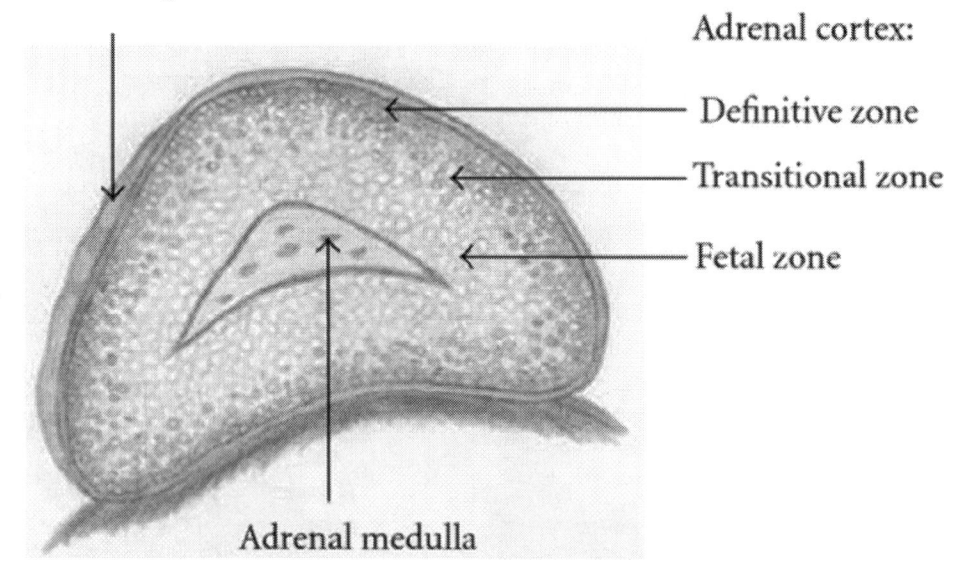

Adrenal cortex:
- Definitive zone
- Transitional zone
- Fetal zone

Adrenal medulla

What you perceive and what you practice does not become a mental matter, but it becomes a matter of biological reception which leads to memory, then addiction. What goes in will come out. What goes in will be birthed into reality. Notice in the adrenal gland that there is a fetal zone. Every thought is transferred into an immediate existence by the adrenal gland. This is conception that's registered in this zone. Adrenaline is then released with the story of your greatness built into it.

Upon the release of adrenaline or epinephrine, you then become the exception. What do I mean by this? This is the practice of your perception along with the practice of your passion and purpose. You become exceptional at what you do at any level. Let me explain. What most consider to be fear is the body giving you the education and the stamina to be exceptional.

You have the same baker that has an extreme passion for baking. But as he looks at the bakeshop or bakery, he immediately replies, "I cannot afford to do such a thing.". Is this true? No. They have become an immediate liar to their own passion and purpose. They shut down their own reality. Do they really need to own a bakery or a bakeshop to practice their passion and purpose?

The answer is no. There's a stove in their kitchen. There are spatulas and spoons in their kitchen. There's countertop space. There is a rolling pin. There's flour. There's sugar. There's cinnamon. Etc. it's all there. Just start!

A renowned psychologist, Dr. Kimbleton Wiggins used the following example to teach his students. He had a volunteer to come to the front of the room and ask them to put their hand directly in front of them. They did. He then instructed them to turn as far as they can to the left and mark the space that they extended out to. Once completed, he asked them to relax and to repeat after him.

"I can turn further."

"I can turn much further."

"I can turn much further than I did before."

Then Dr. Wiggins asked them to proceed to try the exercise again and turn as far as they can to the left with their hands in front of them and mark the space. There was extreme shock in the room, both by the individual who was the subject of the test and the entire classroom. There was an extreme difference in that person's ability to turn much further than he did before.

The point of this exercise was to show that upon the immediate proclamation and the institution of a new perception, it caused the body to react accordingly immediately!!!

Dr. Wiggins then proceeded to the next exercise. He called another student to become the test subject. The student was fantastically excited about the opportunity to do something extraordinary. Dr. Wiggins asked the student, that upon counting to three he wanted the student to touch the ceiling. It was a good 20-foot ceiling. The classroom was enthralled and filled with a heightened sense of anticipation as they truly believed that the student was going to supernaturally jump and touch the ceiling based on the previous exercise. Dr. Wiggins began his count.

"One. Two. Wait for it………………………….. Three!"

The student didn't budge. Based on his perception he did not make a move. Why didn't he jump?

Dr. Wiggins expressed the question, "Why didn't you jump?"

The student responded, "I can't."

Dr. Wiggins said, "Why not?"

The student, "It's way too high."

Dr. Wiggins responded, "I see that. But why did you not touch the ceiling?"

Everyone sat there puzzled. Dr. Wiggins proceeded to walk to the front of the room and grabbed a ladder. Dr. Wiggins said, "This ladder was here the whole time, but you did not open your mind to all the possibilities of touching the ceiling".

In our next exercise we are going to work on the perception that causes conception. The conception that becomes the exception. And the exception that leads to reception, guaranteed. This is how exacting your biological system is.

Perception ➡ Conception ➡ Exception ➡ Reception

When the baker perceives his kitchen as a starting point to bake a few pies in his own kitchen, he is practicing his passion and purpose. There is no excuse for not doing what you want to do right now. Let me make this point. **While you are waiting to practice your passion and purpose, someone else will be practicing it. You can't afford to wait. Waiting is wasting**. Secondly, each moment that you're not practicing your success, then information comes into your body that has nothing to do with where you're going. This is the practice of poverty. Let's move beyond that.

Based on your passion and your purpose, align a short version of your passion and purpose in each space. Be sure to write the same information in both spaces.

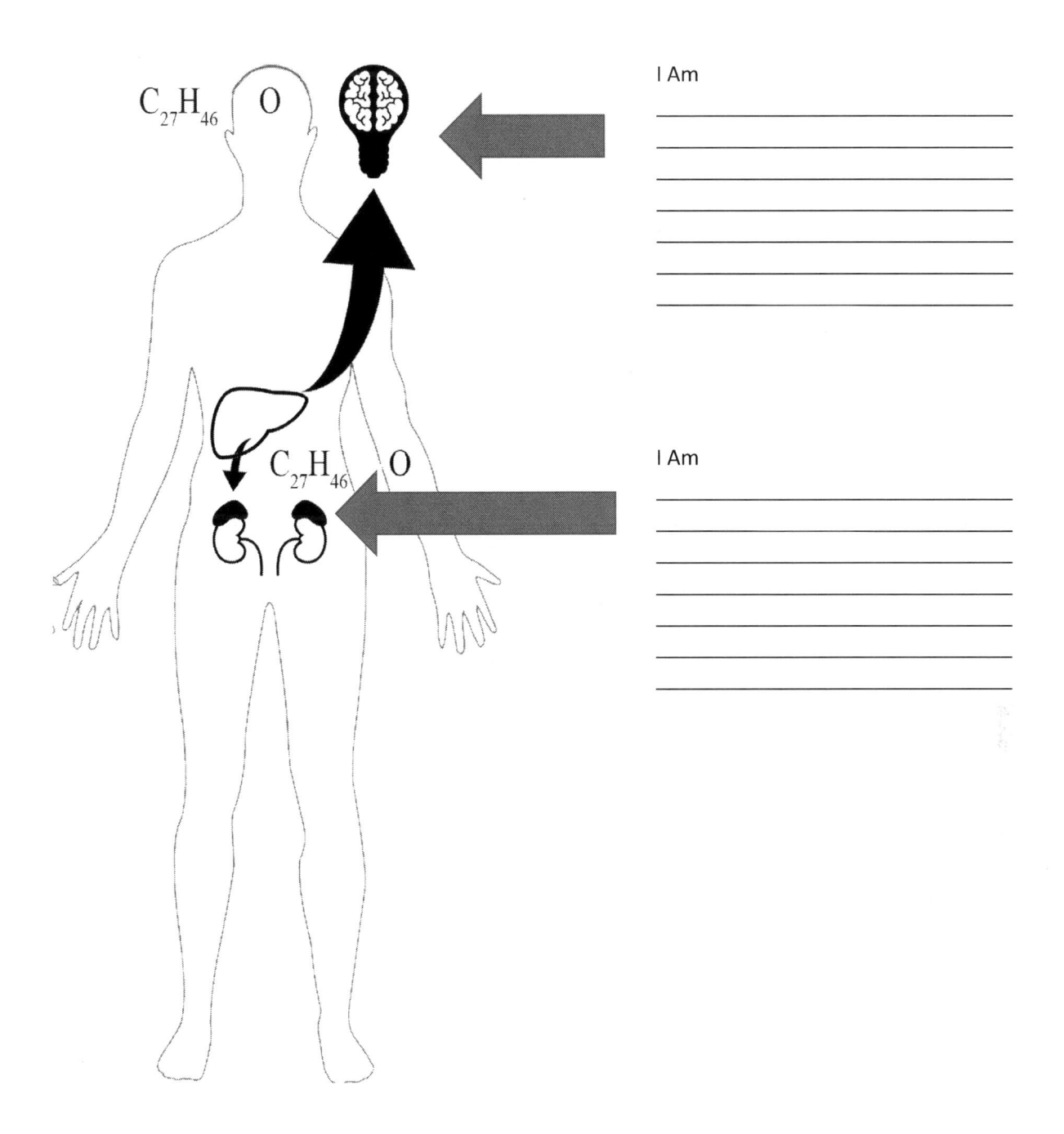

I Am
_____
_____
_____
_____
_____
_____
_____
_____

I Am
_____
_____
_____
_____
_____
_____
_____
_____
_____

Cholesterol flows both to the brain and the adrenal gland to process representations of your perception, words, and actions. But Perception should be the only place where you put the energy of thought.

```
Perception  ←──  Thought Process
    ↓                  ↓
Conception      Brain & Adrenal
                   Adoption
    ↓                  ↓
Exceptional     Actions & Addictions
                And how you show up.
    ↓                  ↓
Reception           Results
```

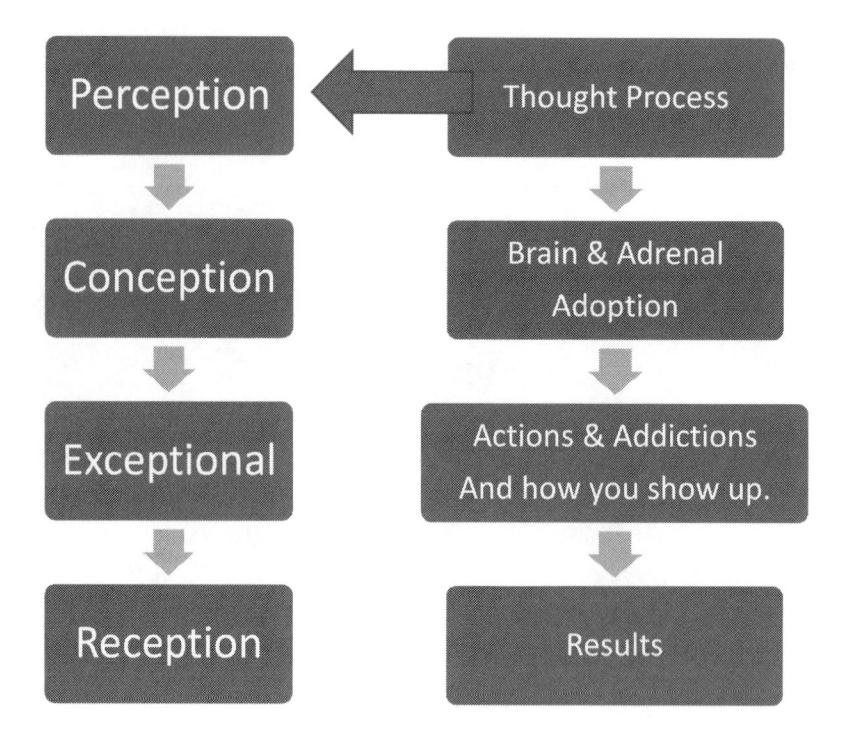

Once again, perception determines how you experience any event, which in turn becomes embedded in your body. Once it's embedded, your future becomes an addiction. This addiction is how you show up in the world, and no matter what you face in terms of situations and circumstances, it does not move you away from your addiction, which in this case is your dream and destiny.

Again, you can predetermine your perception well before any event happens, by the time that event happens, you have shaped the event versus the event shaping you.

Examples

From the baker's standpoint:

When the oven shuts down, they create a bakeless dish, because they have already predetermined that they are the number one baker in the world.

From an artist's standpoint:

All of their brushes are left on the plane. They do their first paintings by hand, which increased the value of their work on the spot.

The list can go on and on. The ability to see who you are beyond any circumstance and situation will give you the actions to take to move beyond. The truth of who you are is always beyond.

List 10 things that you can practice now when it comes to your purpose.

1. _____
2. _____
3. _____
4. _____
5. _____
6. _____
7. _____
8. _____
9. _____
10. _____

These are predetermined actions. Now list the items that's written out in the Passion and Purpose section of your affirmations. It will be the same but in the form of a list.

1. _____
2. _____
3. _____
4. _____
5. _____
6. _____
7. _____
8. _____
9. _____
10. _____

Now list 10 things at least that is happening to you now that you don't like. Be honest with yourself.

1. _____
2. _____
3. _____
4. _____
5. _____
6. _____
7. _____
8. _____
9. _____
10. _____

Now we will look at these 10 things in an entirely different way. Remember, you choose what you see. And if your purpose and passion is deeply rooted in you, something about your purpose and passion will reach back and cause you to see the things that you think you don't like in a completely different way. This is the process of "Reframing". You can find out more about this in Dr. Jada Jackson's book "Reframe".

Reframing Exercise

For item number one, first write down your purpose and passion starting with "I Am". This is the same as what you wrote in order to impact the cholesterol in your body. Then write the thing that you don't like that's happening to you starting with "I Am". What you will immediately notice is that you can't. Your passion and your purpose will not let you. Let me give you an example.

A speaker:

The problem:

The flight to speak to an audience of 500 people was delayed. The event will be over by the time he lands.

Their predetermined affirmation:

I Am the world's greatest speaker. I am speaking to thousands of people consistently, and I am impacting lives every day.

Their initial mix:

I Am the world's greatest speaker. I am speaking to thousands of people consistently, and I am impacting lives every day. I Am on a flight that is delayed, and I will never make the event.

Their corrected mix "Reframed" (Dr. Jada Jackson):

I Am the world's greatest speaker. I am speaking to thousands of people consistently, and I am impacting lives every day. I Am impacting lives (remember), I am impacting the lives on this flight who are also getting to their destinations late.

Reframed Behavior:

"Excuse me everyone, since my flight is delayed and your flight is delayed, can I share what I was to speak on tonight with you right now. The people waiting for me won't get the benefit of this speech, but you can at this very moment."

He speaks and everyone on that flight is emotionally moved. Upon exiting the plane, he received an invitation by a passenger to come speak to an audience of 10,000 people in a couple of months.

For each item on the list of the things that you don't like that's happening to you now, you are going to relist them. But before each item, you will put your initial "I Am" statement. Then list the thing that you don't like starting with "I Am" and reframe what's happening. Usually when you reframe what's happening, you have to take immediate action. So be prepared.

1. I Am _____
   _____

   I Am _____
   _____

2. I Am _____
   _____

   I Am _____
   _____

3. I Am _____
   _____

   I Am _____
   _____

4. I Am _____
   _____

   I Am _____
   _____

5. I Am _____
   _____

   I Am _____
   _____

6. I Am
_____

   I Am
_____

7. I Am
_____

   I Am
_____

8. I Am
_____

   I Am
_____

9. I Am
_____

   I Am
_____

10. I Am
_____

    I Am
_____

This is the practice of changing your perception.

Now list 10 things from your past that is highly troubling to you and you know that it's interrupting your success. Again, be honest with yourself.

1. _____
2. _____
3. _____
4. _____
5. _____
6. _____
7. _____
8. _____
9. _____
10. _____

Once again, write down your authentic affirmation of your passion and purpose, then refrain each item from your past according to your passion and purpose.

1. I Am
   _____
   _____

   I Am
   _____
   _____

2. I Am
   _____
   _____

   I Am
   _____
   _____

3. I Am
   _____
   _____

   I Am
   _____
   _____

4. I Am
   _____
   _____

   I Am
   _____
   _____

5. I Am
   _____
   _____

   I Am
   _____
   _____

6. I Am
   _____
   _____

   I Am
   _____
   _____

7. I Am
   _____
   _____

   I Am
   _____
   _____

8. I Am
   _____
   _____

   I Am
   _____
   _____

9. I Am
   _____
   _____

   I Am
   _____
   _____

10. I Am _____
   _____

   I Am _____
   _____

Past events are merely current events stored in your body. Although these things have happened in the past, they are current because they are memory. You can take any memory and design it to accord with your purpose and your passion. That's the gift that you are given as a human being.

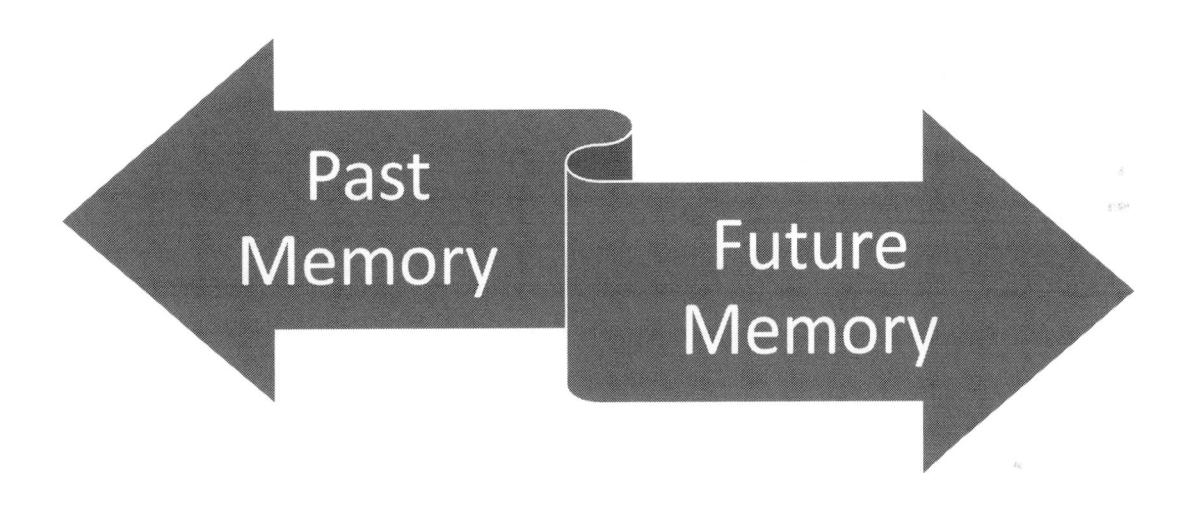

Past Memory ← → Future Memory

You cannot erase the past memory that you don't like or the memory that doesn't serve you, but you can look at those exact past events or circumstances and see it from an entirely different perception. This is where you can rewire your addictions that don't serve you. Every bad thing, every wrong thing, and every dark thing that has happened to you in the past can contribute to your future.

These are a few ways of determining your future and reframing events and your past to make them match.

Thing to Remember

1. When you choose to determine your future based on past circumstances, situations, and events, it becomes a lie toward your future.
2. Your greatest potential, your greatest purpose, your greatest passion, and your greatest place in life is your actual truth.
3. Keep the past from affecting your future, you must make choices about your future and what comes next in your life.
    a. The entirety of your subsequent actions matches the new choices of your future.
    b. Your relationships must be built in accordance with the new choices of your future
4. If you're not getting consistent results towards what you want, or there is a constant struggle towards accomplishment and you do not have an extreme sense of fulfillment, then there is a lie in told somewhere. You are being dishonest with the truth of who you can become.
5. Become your own greatness.

Conception

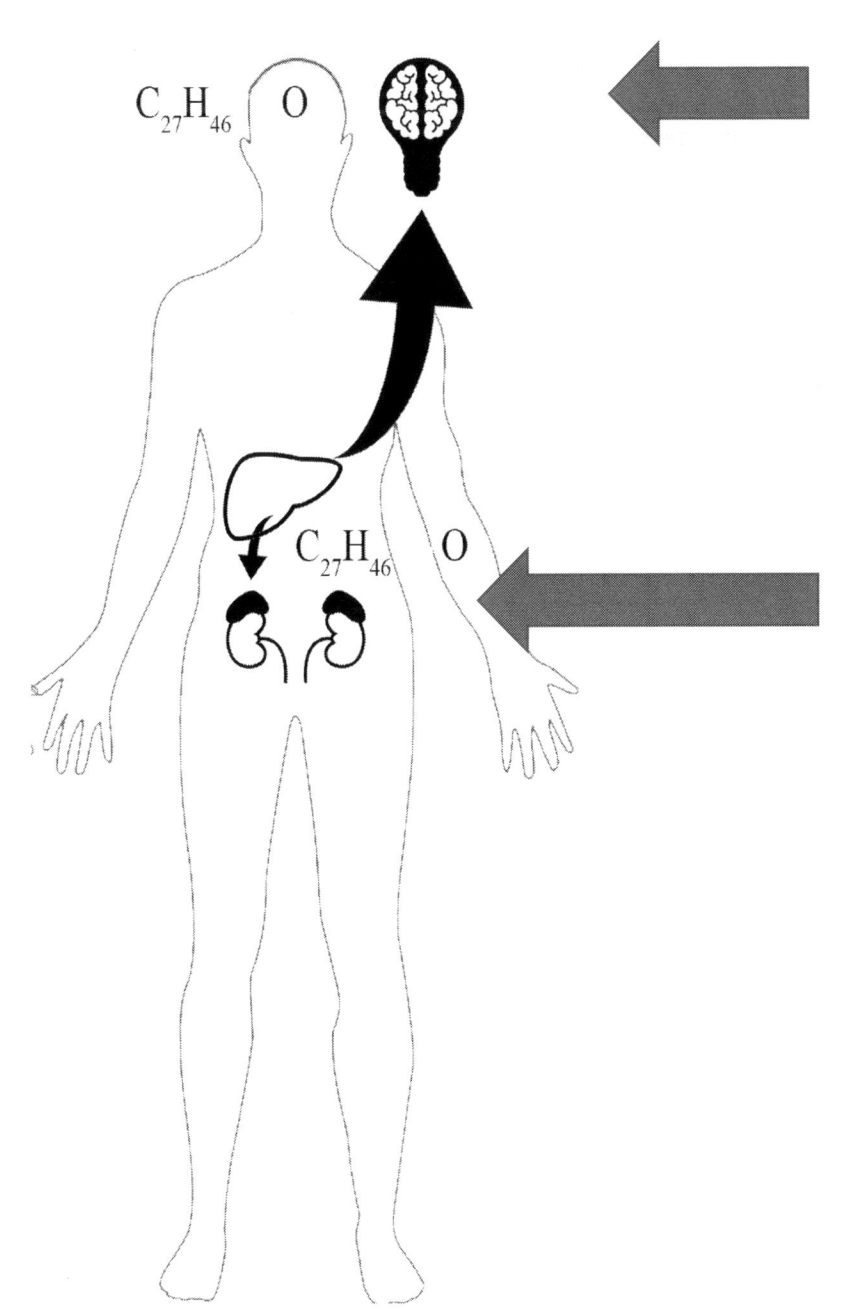

$C_{27}H_{46}O$

$C_{27}H_{46}O$

Your "I Am" extends here via cholesterol flowing through the blood stream to your brain. This is your ideas, your passions, and your purpose. Your cholesterol breaks up at a barrier that protects the brain, passes through that barrier and then reforms as a neuron mirroring what you want.

Your "I Am" also flows here by means of cholesterol also. It pierces the adrenal gland through the 3 layers of your adrenal gland. First converting into a mineral salt, then converting into a sugar which is the memory of what you want. It lastly converts into a sex hormone that excites an adrenaline release that carries the education of what you want, not fear. Within this space is also a sex hormone for life accomplishments and a fetal space for the birth of what you want.

Exception or Exceptionalism

When you set your perception to where it sufficiently impacts your adrenal gland and the neurons, when it is thusly conceived, you then become the exception to failing principles. Everything you do will automatically be done at another level. You will be different. You will see things different. You will do things differently. You will do things on a level that most people can't even begin to do. **When everybody says no I can't, you become the exception**. *At the end of your story you are winning, and not making excuses*. While others are figuring things out, you are done and moving on to what's next. When your perception is conceived, you become exceptional.

1. How You See Things (Perception)
2. Your Every Action (Exception and Exceptional)

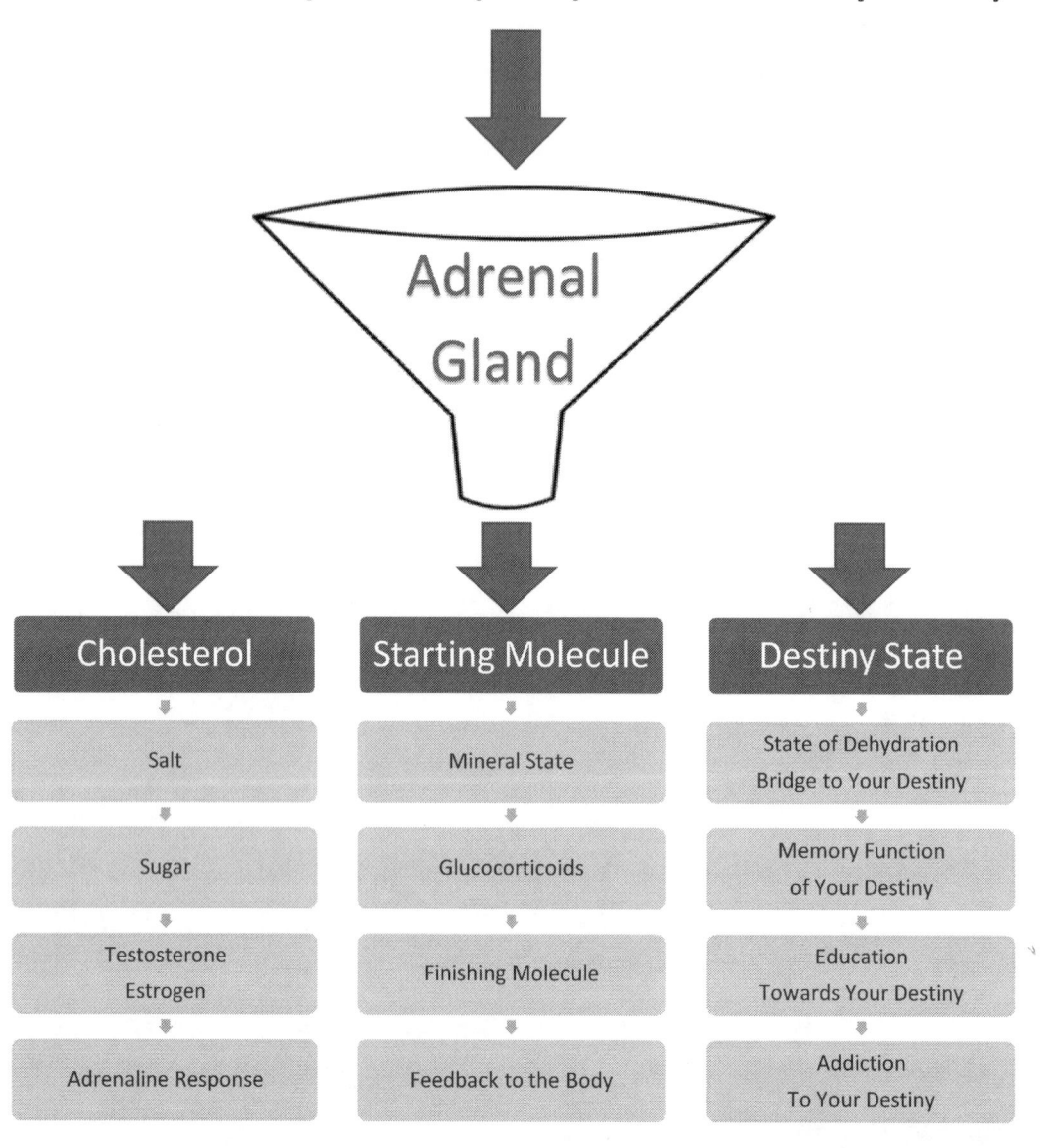

⬇

Adrenal Gland

⬇ ⬇ ⬇

Cholesterol	Starting Molecule	Destiny State
Salt	Mineral State	State of Dehydration / Bridge to Your Destiny
Sugar	Glucocorticoids	Memory Function of Your Destiny
Testosterone / Estrogen	Finishing Molecule	Education Towards Your Destiny
Adrenaline Response	Feedback to the Body	Addiction To Your Destiny

Exceptional practice makes exceptional memory. ***Exceptional memory creates undeniable addictions***. You must create the energy or an insatiable appetite for what you want. So, if you are looking for exceptional results, there must be exceptional activity at all times.

You must be clear about the fact that your personal biological chemistry will follow the level of your intent. It will mirror the level of your intent. The science of your body is exacting, and you must be careful how you feed it. Again, ***your behavior patterns will always launch off of how you feel***. This is why most people can't change their minds; their feelings are in an old place.

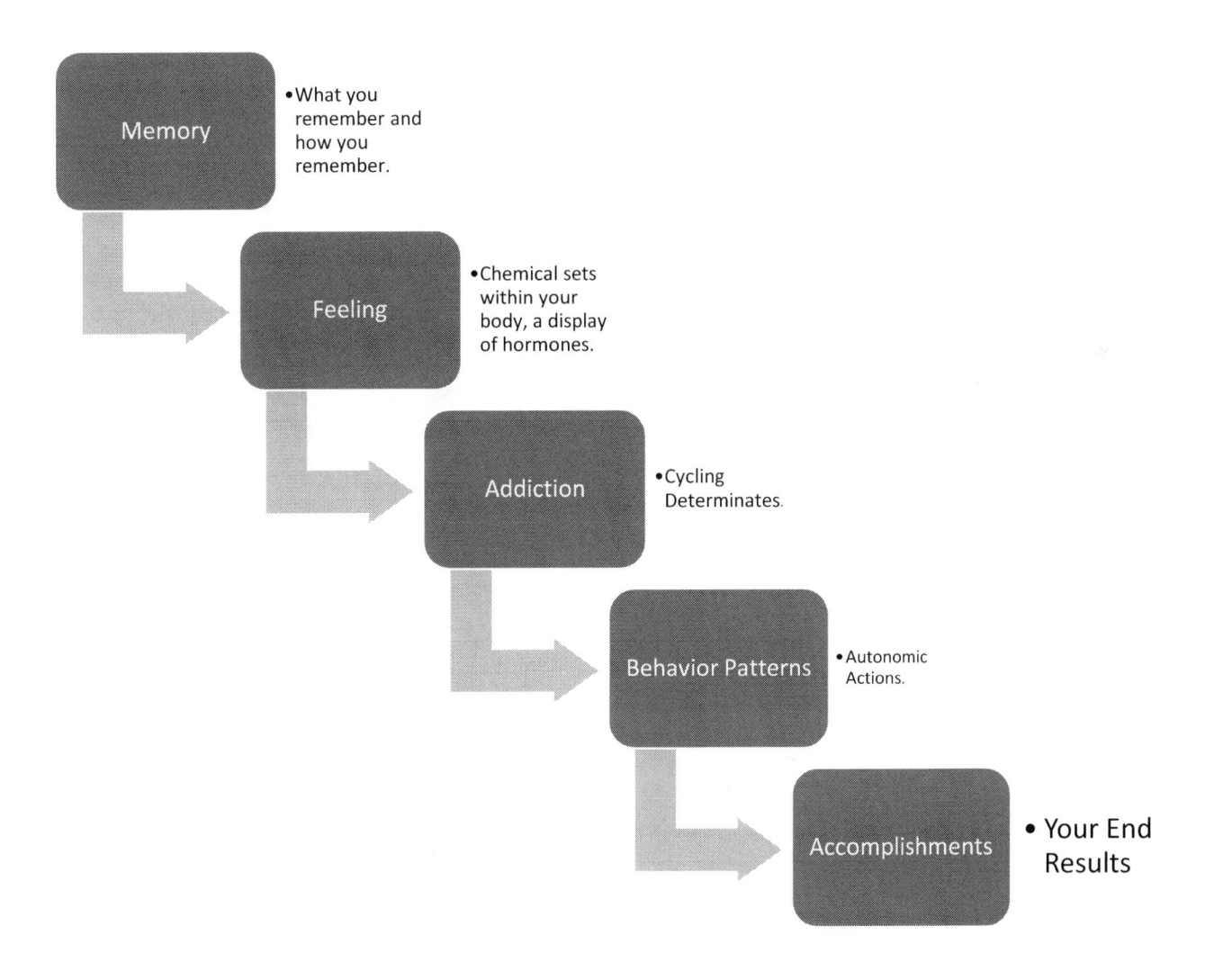

- **Memory** — What you remember and how you remember.
- **Feeling** — Chemical sets within your body, a display of hormones.
- **Addiction** — Cycling Determinates.
- **Behavior Patterns** — Autonomic Actions.
- **Accomplishments** — Your End Results

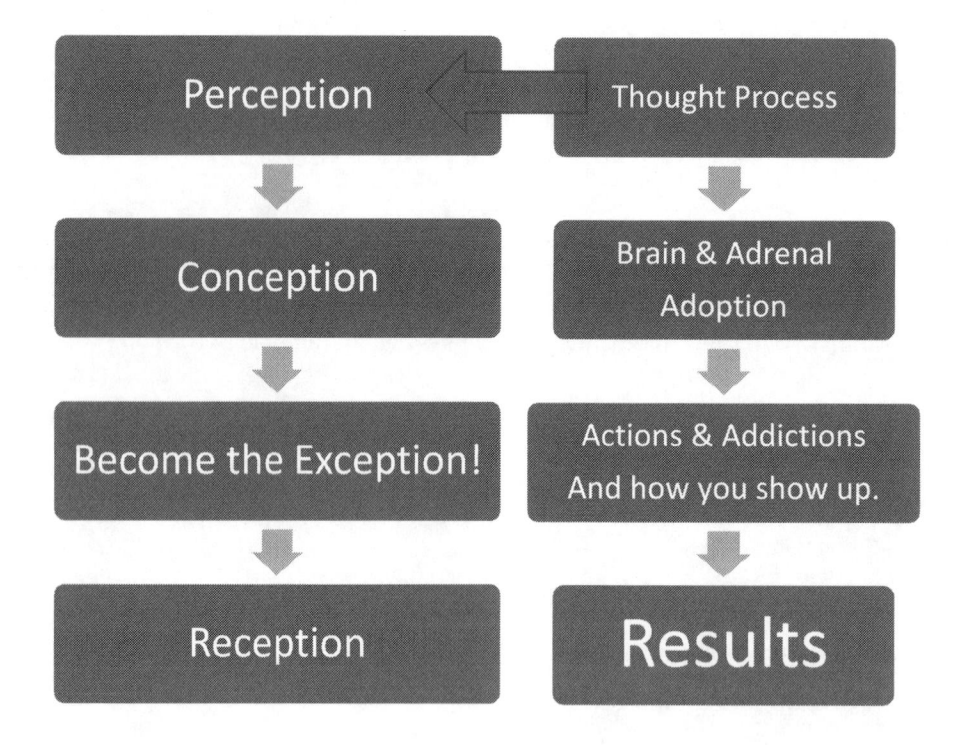

```
Perception  ⇄  Thought Process
    ↓                ↓
Conception     Brain & Adrenal
                  Adoption
    ↓                ↓
Become the      Actions & Addictions
Exception!      And how you show up.
    ↓                ↓
Reception         Results
```

To complete this exercise, go back to where you have mapped out your perception. Again, here's where you do your thinking. You apply your thinking to your perception. Yes, you plan out what you want to remember. And as you come up on different circumstances, your memory will take over. Here's where you need to document your results or what is received.

First, let's note the level in which you will act. Take the list of the things that you said that you can do now. You will convert this list to know how you would do the very thing at an exceptional level. Remember that the baker who could only see himself as employed. There is a baker who saw himself owning. Then there was a baker who **remembered** he was a superstar. Turn your actions into exceptional actions. What are you willing to do different and what are you willing to do greater? What is it that no one else is doing?

1. _____

   Now what's the exceptional action?
   _____
   _____

2. _____

   Now what's the exceptional action?
   _____
   _____

3. _____

   Now what's the exceptional action?

   _____
   _____

4. _____

   Now what's the exceptional action?

   _____
   _____

5. _____

   Now what's the exceptional action?

   _____
   _____

6. _____

   Now what's the exceptional action?

   _____
   _____

7. _____

   Now what's the exceptional action?

   _____
   _____

8. _____

   Now what's the exceptional action?

   _____
   _____

9. _____

   Now what's the exceptional action?

   _____
   _____

10. _____

    Now what's the exceptional action?

    _____
    _____

Reception

Reception is also autonomic. You receive at the level you perceive. Here you must document the results in your life. You have to take measurement to assure that you're on the right path. If things don't turn out the way you expect them to, then you can go back to determine your perception and the resulting actions. List your results in the following spaces.

Use this space to document your results as they happen. Don't lie to yourself. Include everything. Include the date. Sign it as a gesture of responsibility. If it's not what you want, take responsibility.

1. _____
   Date_____   Signature_____
2. _____
   Date_____   Signature_____
3. _____
   Date_____   Signature_____
4. _____
   Date_____   Signature_____
5. _____
   Date_____   Signature_____
6. _____
   Date_____   Signature_____
7. _____
   Date_____   Signature_____
8. _____
   Date_____   Signature_____
9. _____
   Date_____   Signature_____
10. _____
    Date_____   Signature_____

Here's what you are doing?

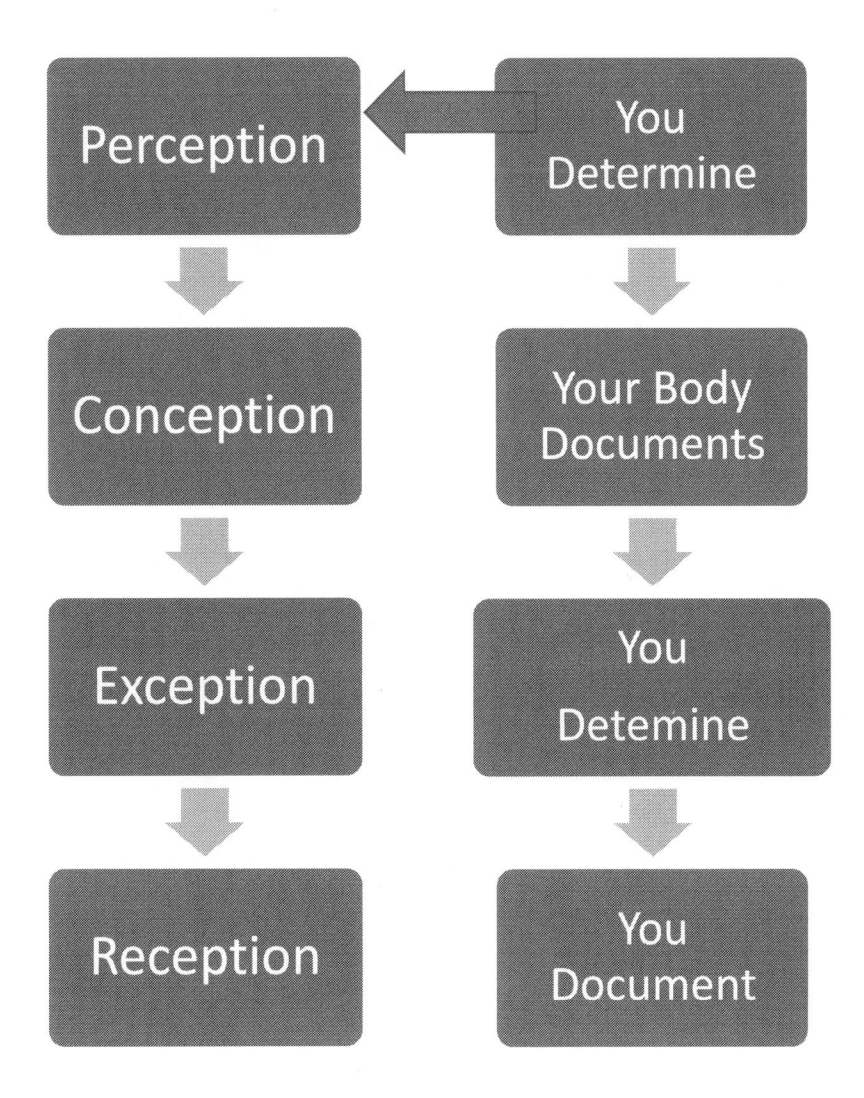

```
Perception  ←——  You Determine
    ↓                ↓
Conception       Your Body Documents
    ↓                ↓
Exception        You Detemine
    ↓                ↓
Reception        You Document
```

The Energy of Your Relationships

In the previous section we covered the energy of the adrenal gland and it's contribution to your memory as it concerns your destiny, purpose and passion, and your choice towards your own greatness. We also covered the fact that your success parameters are uploaded to your brain via the movement of cholesterol towards your brain. The space of your brain that's impacted by optimal cholesterol is the hippocampus and hypothalamus. That which rings or registers in the hippocampus automatically rings and registers in the hypothalamus. From here, the hypothalamus releases a hormone to the pituitary gland, which in turn activates the following three hormones in the pituitary gland.

Growth Hormone
Vasopressin
Oxytocin

It is the Vasopressin and Oxytocin hormones that I want to focus on. But in addition, you must know that the Hypothalamus, the Pituitary gland, and the Adrenal gland are intimately related as they release a chain reaction that is vital towards your personal success. Vasopressin and Oxytocin impacts the adrenal gland and its processes.

Vasopressin
Oxytocin

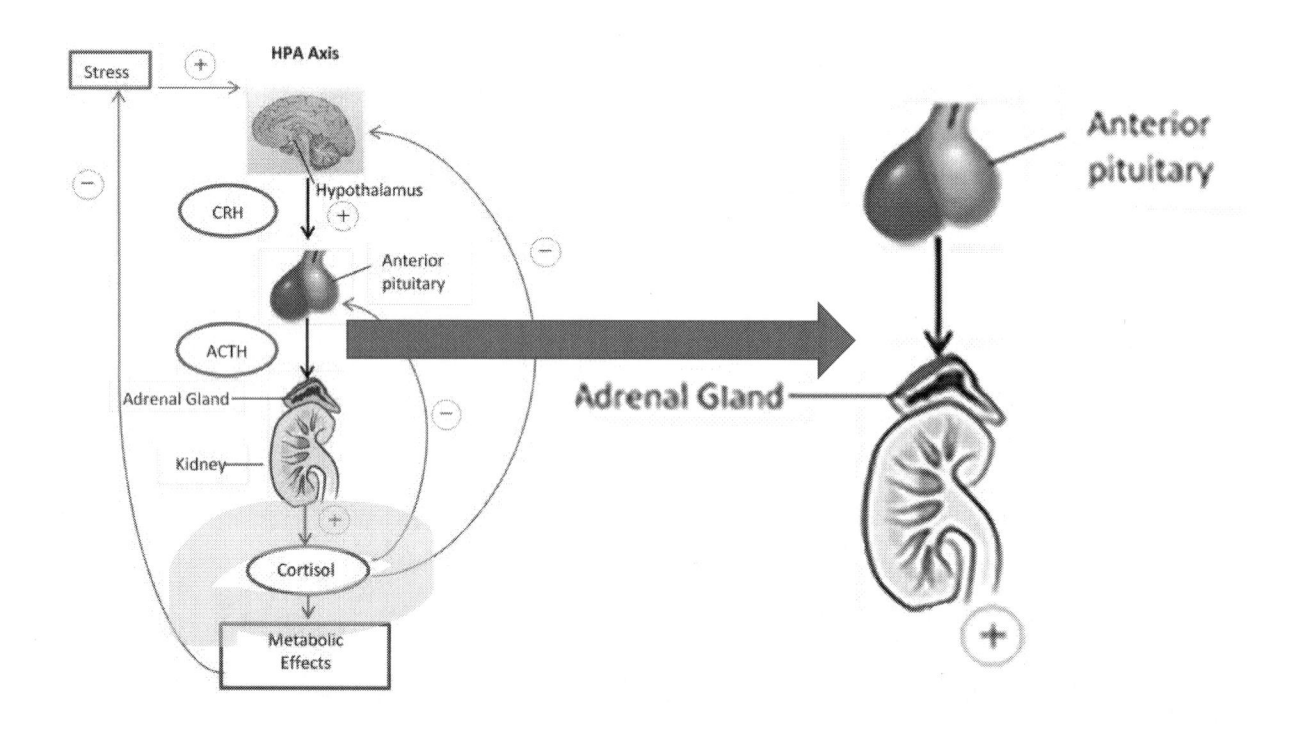

56 | Page

All of this might look a little crazy to you, but I will clean it up until it makes perfect sense. I must include this diagram to include medical personal, biologist, and other scientist who might be concerned about the accuracy of this information. The diagram above emphasizes Cortisol movement towards the bottom which is the steroid hormone (circled above). Cortisol is considered to be a stress related hormone as it responds to stressful situations. The amount of this hormone produced is relative to the amount of stress or pressure you might be facing at any given moment as it reports back to the brain a state of being.

The diagram below focuses on another hormone created in the adrenal gland, glucocorticoids, which is also a steroid hormone. Much like cortisol, it also reports back to the brain a state of being. As you can clearly see, is that both hormones feed back to the hypothalamus and the pituitary gland.

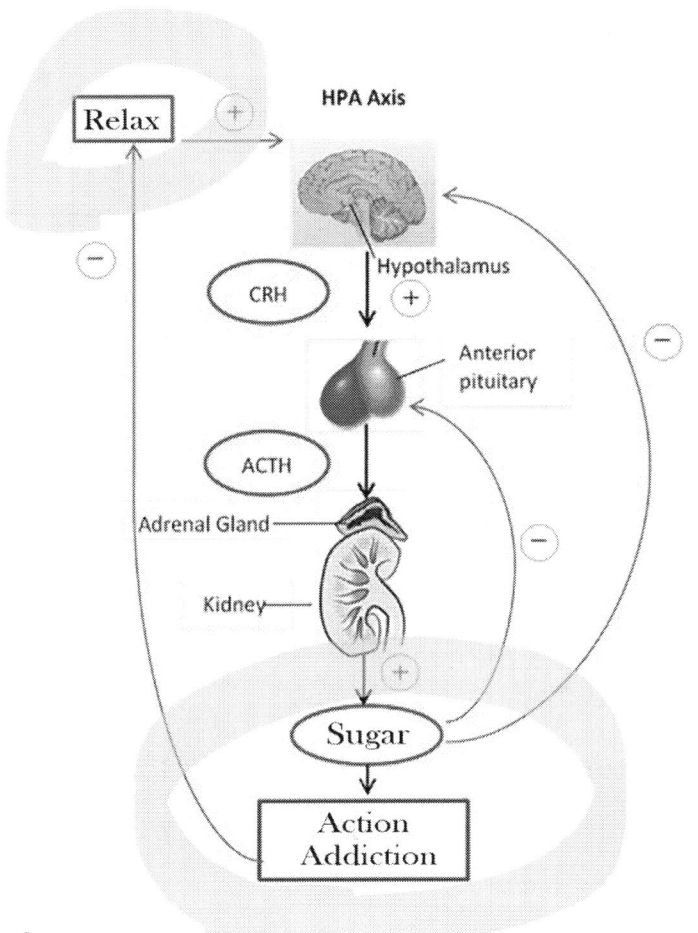

Why is this important?

Remember, sugar is a function of memory. This memory reports back to the pituitary gland. You also must remember that once memory is set in, your actions will flow without any assistance or an attempt to make a decision or a determination on your actions. Simply, once something is set in your body, the actions become inevitable and imminent. It even becomes near impossible to change your mind after that. This is the power of the addictive nature of the body.

Why do people do somethings over and over again and can't seem to possess the will power to make a change? It is the body that makes up the mind. This is why drugs and music are so powerful, they both bypass the processes of the brain and invest itself straight into the body. At this point, it becomes entirely impossible to make a decision otherwise. You run entirely off of memory.

You do what you remember to do, not what you decide to do...

This is why you must make an effort to impact the memory to determine your decisions. You must impact the sugar or glucocorticoids (steroid hormone), because this memory shoots back at your brain like bullets, forcing you to act on the memory. These same pictures are hitting the pituitary gland as a feedback loop.

Why?

There are two hormones that your pituitary gland produces that I want to focus on.

Vasopressin
Oxytocin

These hormones are called pairing hormones. What does this mean?

In evolutionary history this is the hormone that assist all species in determining their ability to pair with the same species. Why do you think that's necessary?

If this hormone did not exist, monkeys would mate with giraffes. Turtles would mate with ducks. Alligators would mate with flamingos. Elephants would mate with rhinos. These pairing hormones or mating hormones keeps specie alignment aligned. This is the same reason why humans don't mate with cats and dogs, llamas, ostriches, or tigers. These hormones help make that determination.

On a secluded island out in the ocean, scientists have studied a species of birds wherein the scientist were able to see and document the evolutionary advancement within a short enough period of time which enabled them to document their findings. It was a specie of birds with brown feathers and black bellies. Towards the middle of the island, they documented the same species with black feathers and black bellies. On the far end of the island, they documented birds with black feathers and brown bellies. What they learned was that the birds with black feathers and brown bellies did not mate with the birds with brown feathers and black bellies.

To continue the advancement of their species, the birds with black feathers and brown bellies are at the far end of the evolutionary chain. To mate with the birds on the other side of the island would cause them to regress in their development. Why is this?

Once a species makes an advancement, it does not go back. This is the work of the hormones, vasopressin and oxytocin, which keeps the species aligned with forward progression. This is exactly the place and space wherein you can make an advancement towards your personal success.

There is a distinct reason why these hormones still function within your pituitary glands. It is still for mating, bonding, and partnering purposes. Why is this important?

Humans have the unique ability to continue to advance beyond their physiological progression. Once the human body matures based off of hormonal development, a human can still mature well beyond physiological development.

A horse is a horse, and primarily does horse things.

A dog is a dog, and primarily does dog things.

Duck is a duck, and primarily does duck things.

A roach is a roach, and primarily does roach things.

A housefly is a fly, and primarily does things that flies do.

An ant is an ant, and primarily does the things that ants do.

A lemon tree is a lemon tree produces lemons.

An orange tree is an orange tree and produces oranges.

A tomato plant is a tomato plant and it produces tomatoes.

I'm sure you get the point.

Everything in evolutionary existence and evolutionary history has a stopping point which serves its purpose. Its passion is basically singular in nature. Every human bypasses a singular event of capability. The hormones in humans spends its time growing the human body to a very specific point. Then the same hormones convert its use towards human accomplishment based on human choice.

Humans do not have an evolutionary stopping point, but can continue to grow into doctors, lawyers, contractors, astronauts, presidents, nurses, teachers, electricians, janitors, inventors, and much more. The same hormones that pushes the advancement and growth of the human body, now contribute to your personal design. But when you do not have a personal design, your hormones then pass on insufficient information to your cells. This is the primary foundation for disease.

A fish remains a fish. A giraffe remains a giraffe. A monkey remains a monkey. There are two amino acids, which are the building blocks of the human body, that separates humans from monkeys. A monkey will remain a monkey its entire life, but a human can move on to be a multiplicity of things based on desire. Within these two amino acids are the capacity to grow into anything possible without limitation. Not having a future desire, a future destiny, a passion and a purpose, leaves you mentally in a primal "monkey" state.

You are designed for greatness, so you must desire greatness. When you are repeating the same life every day, you are admitting that you are incapable of advancing to greater evolutionary states It took billions of years to design most species, as newer species are able to push themselves to the next level in shorter spans of time. The gift that you have, is that you can push to a new level within the moment of a single thought, and then become that. Isn't that amazing?

But what stands in the way of advancement? I'm glad you asked.

You must be fair to your pituitary gland, the gland that stores the "pairing hormones". Humans are the only species in the entirety of evolutionary history that can advance, but can also then go backwards evolutionary wise based on who they pair with, or in essence, based on their connections. We're the only species that can determine to move forward but connect with somebody that does not exist in the same space of desire and destiny selection.

The pituitary gland is abused because we ignore the information that is fed back to it. The natural progression of things disables an advanced species to go back and mate with the previous form of that species.

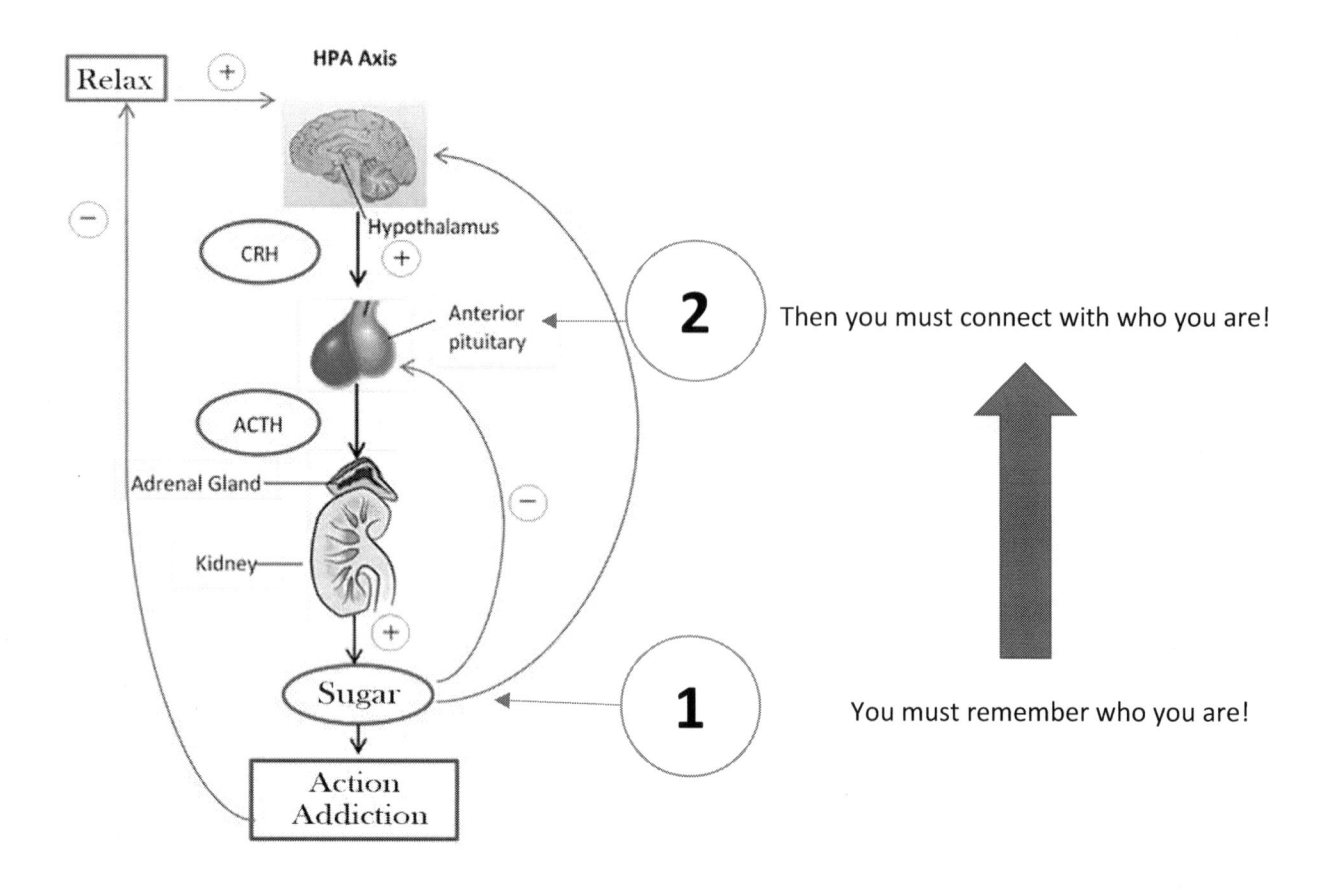

HPA Axis

2 — Then you must connect with who you are!

1 — You must remember who you are!

You must remember who you are, then you must connect to who you are. Once, you decide to be exceptional, you must then connect with those who carry that exception. You must match and mate with those who are of like kind. The hormones vasopressin and oxytocin will push for you to mate with the proper species by blocking out what's not like you.

You must document when you move into your next or new space of existence. You are no longer the same animal, so to speak. ***Once you have determined and have gained clarity on your destiny and that becomes a future memory, you must now in a sense, mate, partner, and connect on that level***. To understand this better, look at the concept of ImbueSynthesis developed by Dr. Milton Howard Jr.

ImbueSynthesis

PhotoSynthesis

ImbueSynthesis
Investment

9 then 1
ooooooooo Glycolysis

Krebs/Electron Transport Chain

= The Substance of your Desire!

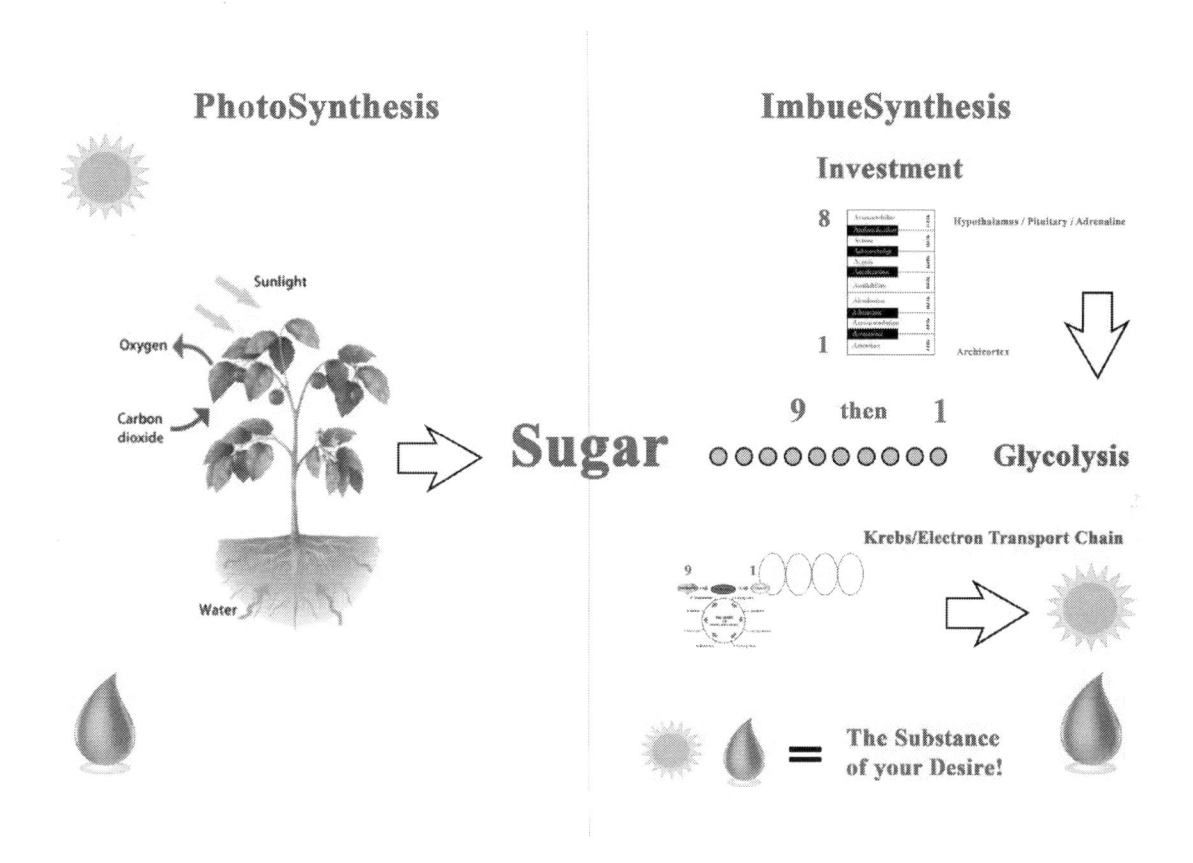

Don't let this diagram scare you. ImbueSythesis is one of the most fascinating concepts in biological truth that you will come across. But first, let me define ImbueSynthesis for you.

ImbueSynthesis – is the quality of investments extending from your personal connections.

To really understand ImbueSynthesis, we must cover photosynthesis, which the exact reverse of ImbueSynthesis.

PhotoSynthesis

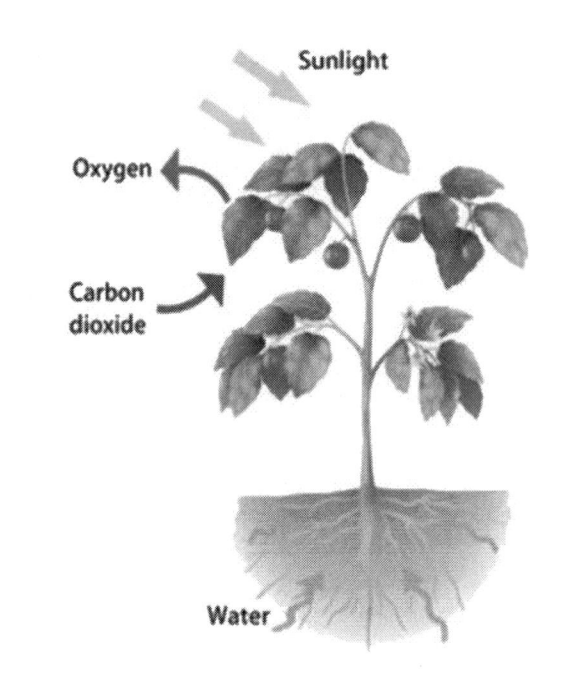

Essentially, photosynthesis is the "light and water" that's invested into vegetation in order for it to become what it is. You must also know that vegetation takes in carbon dioxide and releases oxygen. Let's break it down.

1. Light and water converts a plant or tree from a "seed state" to a "fruit state" or "finishing state".
2. Plants and trees take in carbon dioxide along with light and water.
3. These are essentially investments.
4. Essentially a plant or tree cannot be what it is without light, water, and carbon dioxide.

It is extremely important to note here in addition, that when you look at a plant or tree, the entirety of its makeup is water. You can stick a bamboo plant in the sunlight in a bowl or bucket of water, and you will see that bamboo plant grow into a bamboo tree. Nothing was added to the bowl or bucket aside from just water. What you see in the plant or tree is the conversion of water into a purposeful existence. This is true for all vegetation. Even a giant oak tree is simply converted water. The oak tree does not take the substance from the ground to become the tree, only the water that goes into the ground.

All of this extends from the investment of light, water, and carbon dioxide. Amazing isn't it?

Let's get to the next major point about photosynthesis.

What's in the seed is equivalent to the final production of what's outside of the seed.

SEED = Converting Water

Everything that's in the seed is also in the plant. **What's in the seed is the memory of what the plant will be**. When the plant is fully matured, it is a physical representation of the memory that is contained in the seed. Essentially, when you see the final production of what was+ the seed, you are witnessing a physical manifestation of memory. A plant, a tree, grass, bushes, or any other type of vegetation, once it reaches its matured state, its existence is what it remembers to be. You must vehemently understand this part of photosynthesis.

🌱 = **Memory**

When you look at a fruit tree, a tomato plant, an oak tree, or any other type of vegetation, what you're looking at is memory. *If you want to know what's in a seed, you must start with the investment of water*. Once that seed germinates, it takes in the investment of light and carbon dioxide. When the vegetation matures, *you are witnessing the physicality of memory*. It is the existence of the tree that gives the picture of what's in the seed. None of this happens, or memory does not happen without light, water, and carbon dioxide.

Here is the next point. This is essential photosynthesis 101.

All vegetation is simply a form of sugar. The molecular structure of trees, plants, grasses, or any other type of vegetation is a formation of sugar.

🌱 = **Sugar**

If I were to make a mathematical equation of photosynthesis, it will look like this.

Sugar = Memory

Ah Ha!!! This is the exact biological representation of the function of sugar in your body, memory. Evolutionary wise, vegetation precedes animals and humans. The function of sugar as memory is the exact point of photosynthesis. In addition, *memory always produces a physical manifestation of what it is*. This is also the point of photosynthesis, memory moving from a mere picture to an actual existence. Long before humans existed, memory has been practicing on becoming. As memory moves from the seed, when you add water, the water converted is a version of the seed, but now in the state of the finished plant or the fruit thereof. Note this term.

Converted Water

Converted water is also at the center of your personal significance. The kingdom of vegetation, over billions of years has been learning to convert memory into a physical manifestation by converting water. An apple seed fully knows how to convert water into an apple tree. A lemon seed fully knows how to convert water into a lemon tree. A tomato seed fully knows how to convert water into a tomato plant. I'm sure you get the picture. Now let's take a look at ImbueSynthesis.

ImbueSynthesis is the mirrored version of photosynthesis but works in the reverse manner. ImbueSynthesis is a process that works in your body. Opposite of photosynthesis, ImbueSynthesis is the process in which your body in the end, produces light and water. Amazing!

When you look into the mechanical process which takes place in every cell in your body, each cell is producing light and water in the cell's mitochondria. I want to note here in addition, that your biological profile releases carbon dioxide into the air as you breathe. This is the exact reversal of photosynthesis. Vegetation takes in light, water, and carbon dioxide. You release carbon dioxide, and your cells produce light and water.

Another note that you should consider, is that your body is 85% to 95% made up of water. In addition, the backbone of your DNA is sugar. This is a five-carbon sugar that holds together your DNA sequence. Isn't this amazing? Why does your cells produce light and water?
I am extremely glad you asked.

The light and water that is produced in each and every one of your cells becomes the structure of your DNA as it extends from mRNA (messenger RNA). All of it is sugar. **Your DNA is converted water**. There are several processes that precedes the DNA, but you must understand that **your DNA is an extreme function of memory**. Your DNA is who you are physically. But it is much more than that, and I will show you that in a moment. But let me share with you the statement that I will use extensively a little later.

> ***You cannot become who you are without the investment of someone agreeing with who you are and then acting on it.***

ImbueSynthesis is the quality of investments extending from your personal connections. Water, light, and carbon dioxide is a direct investment into the formation of the physicality of vegetation. In the same light, **the quality of investments extending from your personal connections will become the physicality of your highest intentions**. Meaning, you cannot live your dream or experience your dream without the proper investments stemming from your personal connections, much in the same way, wherein a plant or a tree cannot become what it is without sunlight, water, and carbon dioxide. It does not matter what is in the seed in terms of memory, memory is useless without investment.

Let me take the time to extend a side note here for those who are personally experiencing extreme emotional trauma. Emotional trauma is a result of past memories. You keep experiencing those memories as an immediate reality because you surround yourself with people who keep investing or reinvesting those negative events into your body through their words and actions towards you. Check this out.

> ***To change your past experiences,***
> ***you must change your current connections.***

This is not a philosophical statement. This is a physiological statement. Now let's cover the bio-physical points of ImbueSynthesis.

The Hormones

First, your hormones are forms of water that are excreted from a series of glands. These secretions are chemical compositions that have a primary role in what develops within your cells. Hormones is the way that your body communicates with itself. **_Your entire body works off of memory and the messaging of that memory_**. Hormones also interact with each other, giving each other instructions on when to start flowing and sometimes went to stop flowing.

Hormones are molecular chains of information that extends from your DNA via mRNA. They create mirrors. Allow me to explain the importance. Here's what your DNA proves.

Every part of your body is the exact same thing but displays itself as a different expression. Each expression denotes a purpose. Each purpose contributes to the existence of the whole.

The heart and the lung contain the same DNA; therefore, they are the same thing, but expressed differently. The eye and the ear extend from the same DNA code but expresses different purposes. The kidney and the pancreas are the same but coded for different purposes. I am sure you get the point. This is an incredibly simple notion, but it is entirely true. Every organ, every gland, every cell, and tissue are a mirrored version of everything else within your body. The key word here is mirror. Let's start with this unique word – Image. I want to break it up into two parts.

I - Mage

The root of the word image is mage. -mage denotes a specific power of alchemy, which means to transform from one substance to another. If one substance extends as a transformed state from another substance, it is still the previous substance but at a greater level of expression. Yes, you guessed it. Etymology wise, we get the word "magic" from the root – mage. It is also where we get the word magistrate. King. One who by law that carries the power to transform. What is traditionally an image?

It's a reflection. It takes a mirror for the most part to cast a reflection. Keep in mind this phrase –

"Cast A Reflection"

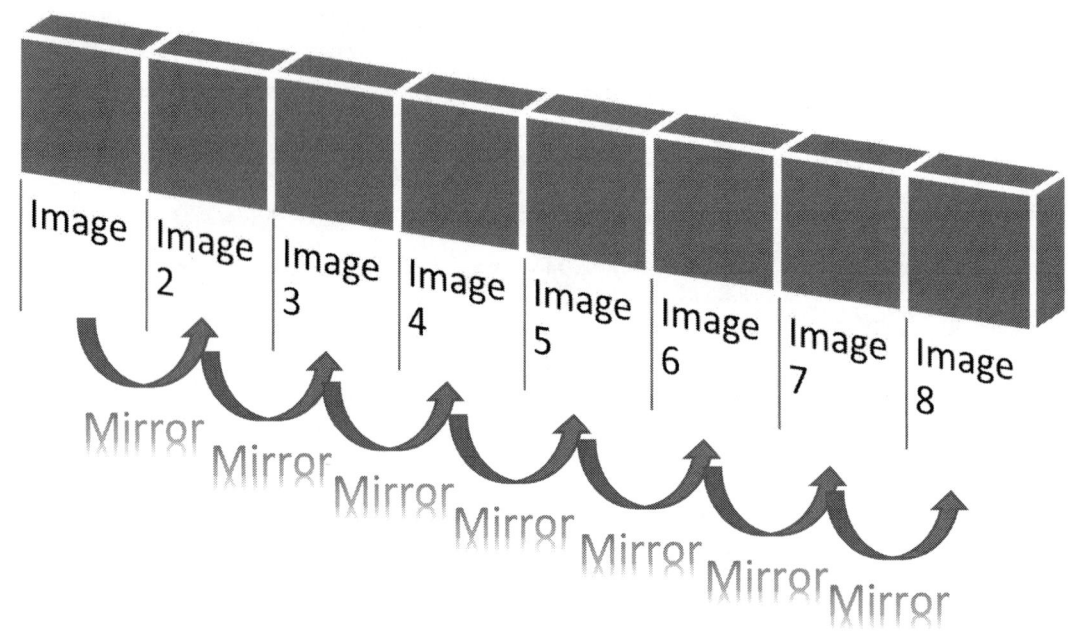

Image 2 is a mirrored version of the original image. Image 3 is a mirrored version of Image 2. Image 4 is a mirrored version of Image 3, and so on. Each one casts a reflection so the next one can exist. When you stand in front of a mirror, you see a casted version of yourself. Allow me to share with you some of the major glands.

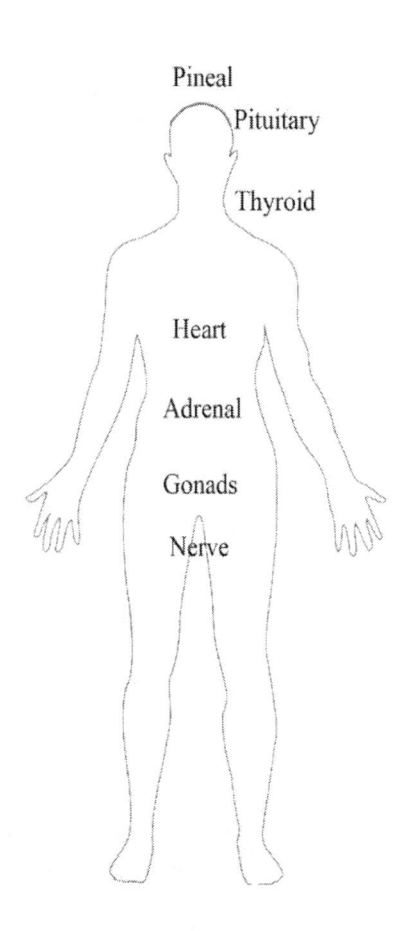

These grands which secrete your hormones are not just an arbitrary existence. These glands are closely interrelated and are designed to cast a reflection outside of your body. These glands are like recorders designed to document your dreams and then accurately cast what you want into existence.

Image   **Image 2**

Mirror

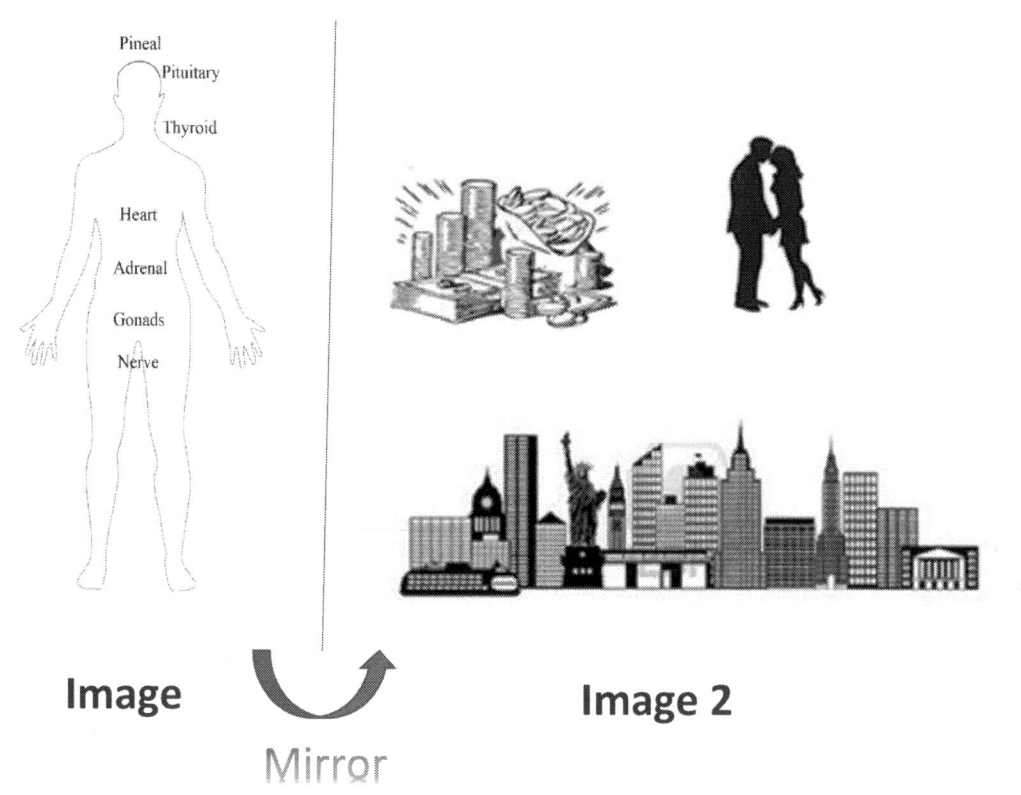

Image 2 is an expression of the original image.

This is a natural conversion. Allow me to explain. Hormones secreting from the glands impact the cells in your body and they also impact each other. Again, their primary function is to communicate or to send messages to multiple parts of your body. The multiplicity of impacts that hormones have, leads to the bottom line of the health of your DNA. Of course, you know that DNA is the blueprint of your body's construction. But **DNA also serves as the blueprint of what you want to accomplish for the future**.

You cannot begin to underestimate the power of the body and its ability to convert not only molecules and compounds, but it is also designed to convert what you want from what can't be seen to what can be seen. This is why it is extremely important to understand the power of the conversions that take place in your body. Especially the conversion of water.

Just as a reminder, the hormones in your body functioned to build who you are from a zygote to a fully formed newborn. Then those same hormones knew exactly what to do to carry you from a newborn to mature adulthood. These hormones do not go into retirement at this point, but *your hormones begin to contribute the energy and the knowledge that you need to accomplish the images that you feed into your body. The body then contributes its vast knowledge of "how to" to assist you in getting the job done*.

CRITICAL PERIODS IN HUMAN DEVELOPMENT*

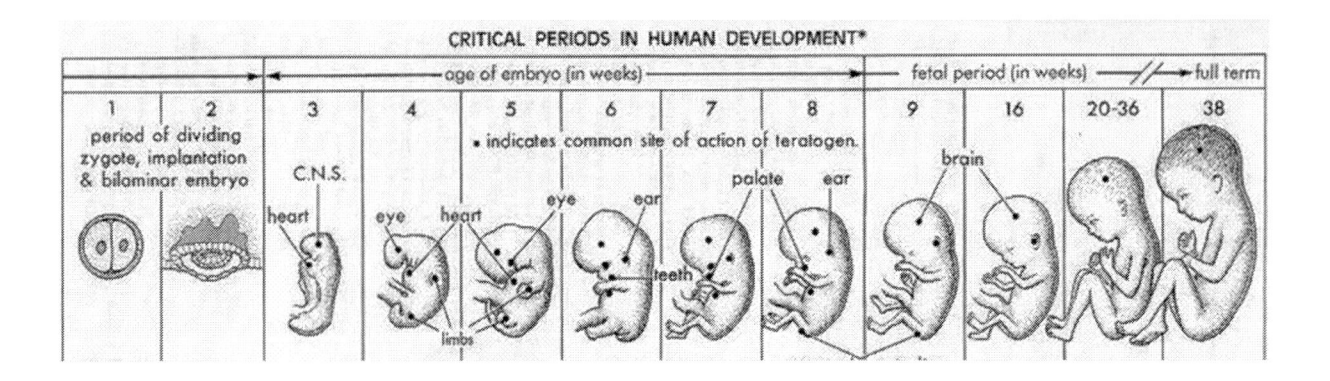

What you see here are not stages of development during a normal human period of gestation. What you see here are points of reflection, imaging, and mirroring. All representations of different expressions at different marked periods of time.

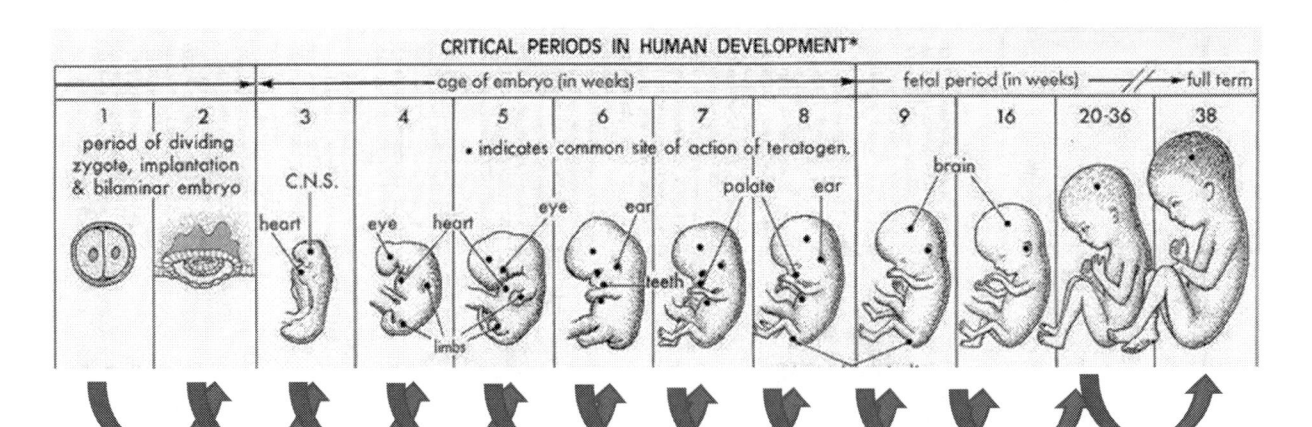

Image 1	Image 2	Image 3	Image 4	Image 5	Image 6	Image 7	Image 8	Image 9	Image 10	Image 11	Image 12

CRITICAL PERIODS IN HUMAN DEVELOPMENT*

Mirror Mirror Mirror Mirror Mirror Mirror Mirror Mirror Mirror Mirror Mirror **Mirror**

Mirror

70 | Page

In the uterus, you see converting water as every stage of embryo development is a mirror of the previous stage. The zygote in the beginning is still the newborn in the end. ***The newborn in the beginning is still the adult human in the end, just a greater expression. What you create in the beginning is still you at the end of creation***. You are just converting what outside of you into something of substance that's already constructed on the inside via memory proliferation. That power is still subject to your body which carries out the initial stages of true alchemy. ***Your accomplishments are the physicality of memory.***

Let's return back to the concept of converting water. A plant is simply water converting upwards, all the while turning into sugar. The formatted sugar is simply a picture of what is remembered. The water converts into the final product of the seed.

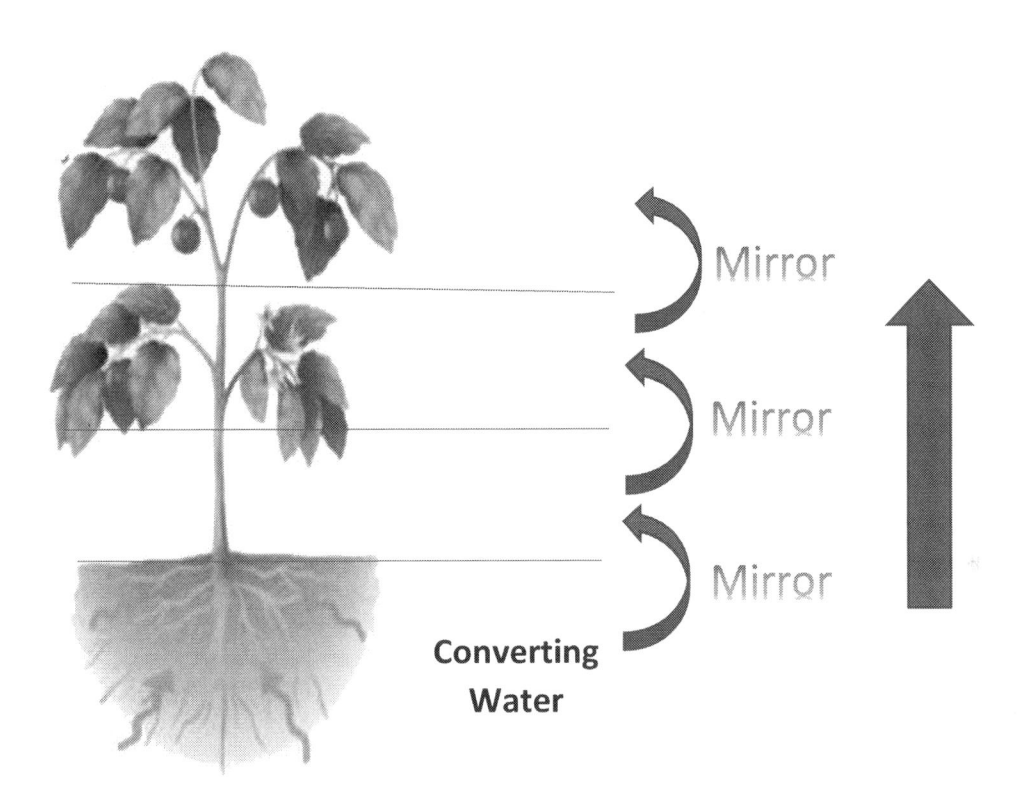

Our bodies essentially behave the same except in a reverse order. Our body takes sugar and converts it into water. This water in our cells is then used to build what we remember to build. Our bodies through a myriad of processes has been practicing building from memory for billions of years. Your body remembers how to build an eye, an ear, a lung, a liver, a kidney and so on. It also has been explicitly trained to build what you decide to build for your future, only if that is the memory that has been instituted.

Physical Memory

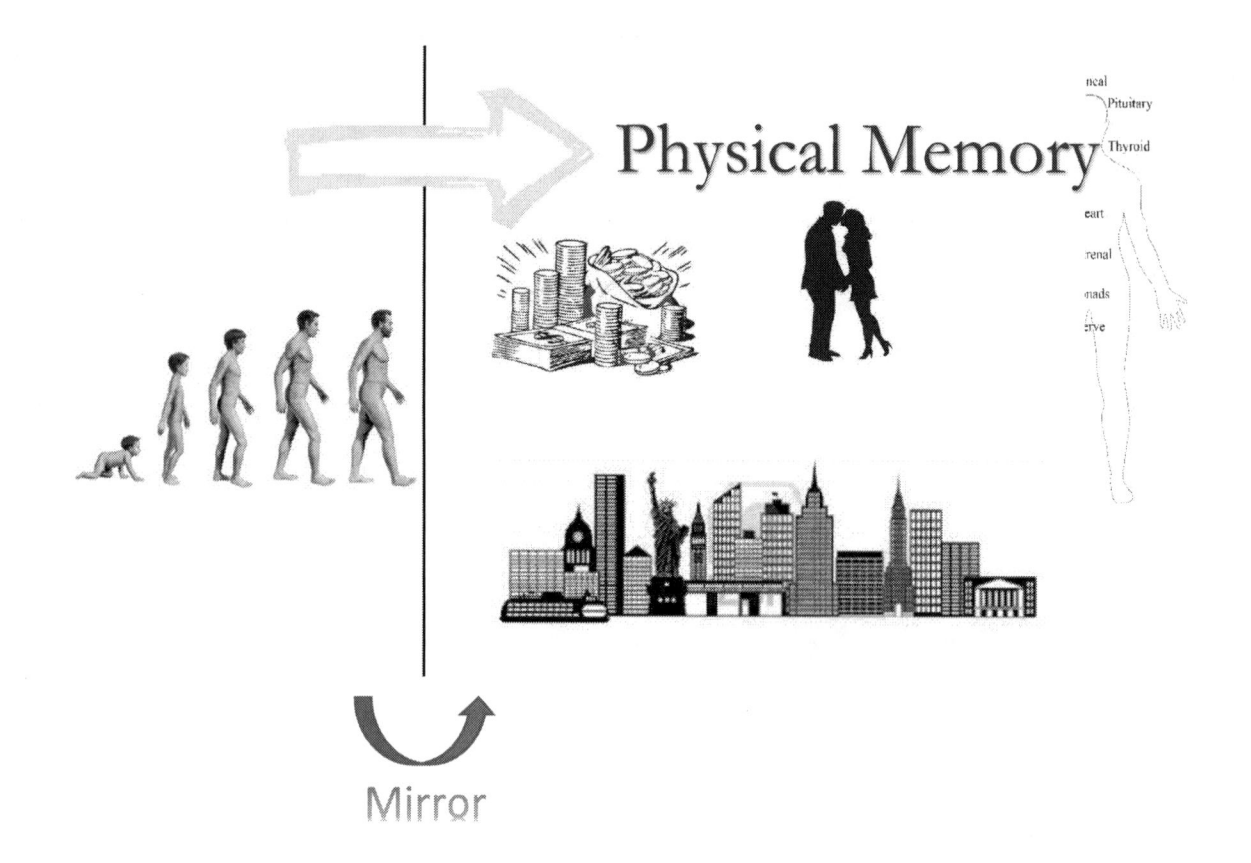

What you create outside of yourself is still a mirror of who you are. If you want to be extremely accurate, the components of who you are mirrors back millions and billions of years. This mirroring technique has been practicing for billions of years, long before your awareness became a part of it

Let's take a look.

Most people understand DNA in two parts. First, the genetic code or sequence, and then secondly, the rest of the DNA sequence.

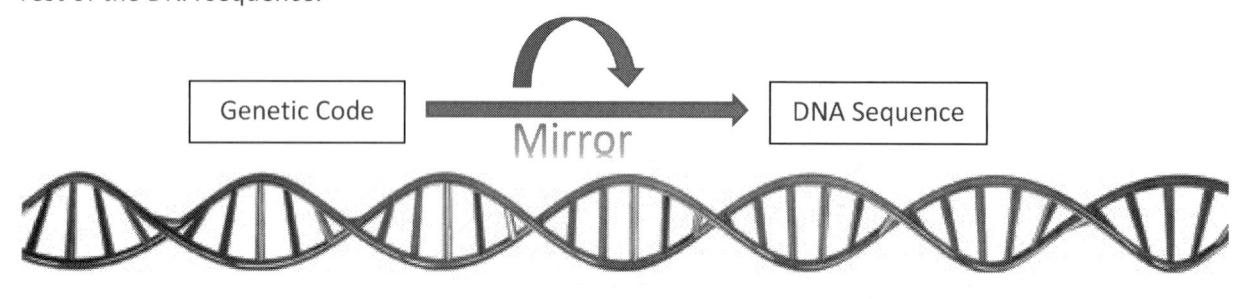

Genetic Code → Mirror → DNA Sequence

Once the genetic code instructs the DNA sequence, then proteins are formed as a result. These proteins become amino acids, which in turn produces the cell communities of the organs and glands. All of this to create and maintain your body in the end.

1 → 2 → 3

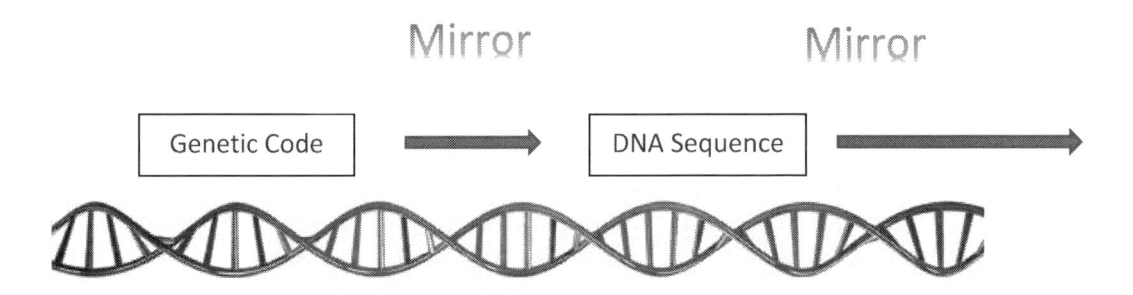

It is the DNA sequence that promote the organization of proteins, which in turn create the amino acids that are the substance of your physical make-up. Here, I want you to think in terms of mirrors. You have glands that secrete the hormones. Then you have the hormones that penetrate the cells. With a few other processes running in between, essentially the hormone impacts the Hormone Response Element. Then the genetic code mirrors the energy of the Hormone Response Element and transfers a direct message to the DNA that extends to the mRNA. The mRNA then creates protein that in turn creates more amino acids. This process exists to instruct the body how to become what it is. It's all just a system of mirrors.

Glands → Hormones → Cell Message → DNA → mRNA → Proteins → Amino Acids → Body Parts

Everything is a mirrored version of everything else. Each resulting stage is just an expression of the previous stage, but still the same thing.

Yes, I am over emphasizing the point. Although you see a different expression at each stage, what is in the end is still the same as what's in the beginning. This entire biological process then transfers over into your outward personal development. **Your passion and your purpose, your lifestyle, the money that you make, and your relationships are mirrored from your physiological expressions**. Although you see a production outside of yourself, it is still who you are on the inside. I cannot emphasize this enough.

Everything here...   Becomes a mirrored version here.

The continuations of production outside of yourself is still who you are. When you accomplish something outside of yourself that you created within yourself, it is an evolutionary advancement.

Therefore, accomplishment is very much a function of biological realities. *Your accomplishments are a* real **force** of life *that reinvest back into you for further accomplishments.*

At its smallest value, the mirroring that takes place in your **DNA** is as exacting as you can get when it comes to the *perfection of repeating accomplishments*. Every part of your body reflects accomplishment at every stage. It is incumbent on you to do the same when it comes to accomplishing your personal greatness. The advantage that you have is a third part of the DNA strand called the Hormone Response Element or HRE.

The Hormone Response Element is influenced by the hormones as it penetrates each of your cells and sends messages to the mitochondria that influences not only your physiological design, but highly *influences how you process your personal accomplishments by impacting the memory of what you want*, which is a component of the five carbon sugar in that is the backbone of your DNA.

The key is the that the hormone response element (HRE) is 100 times more important than genetics. Gene's are influenced by the HRE. The HRE or hormone response element is highly influence by how another person impact you. How another person impacts you has to become an extreme point of focus. This specific impact mirrors directly into your body and can effect the results you are looking for by subtly altering the memory of what you want.

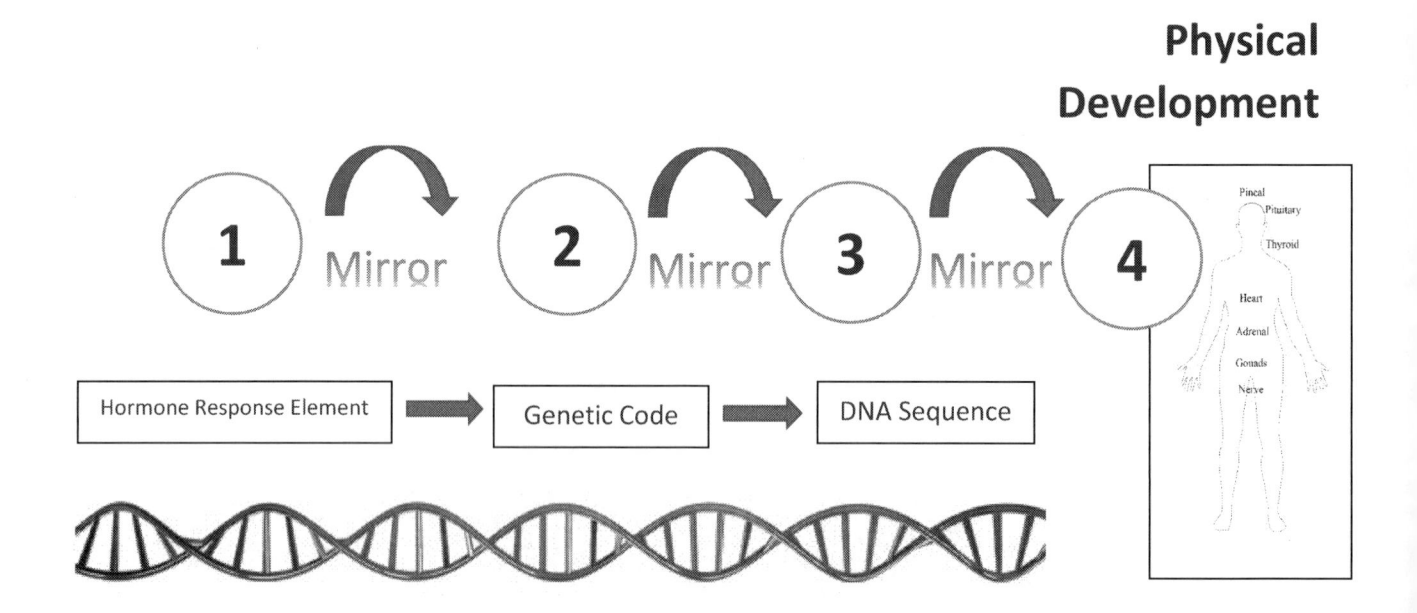

Physical Development

1 → Mirror → 2 → Mirror → 3 → Mirror → 4

Hormone Response Element → Genetic Code → DNA Sequence

Pineal, Pituitary, Thyroid, Heart, Adrenal, Gonads, Nerve

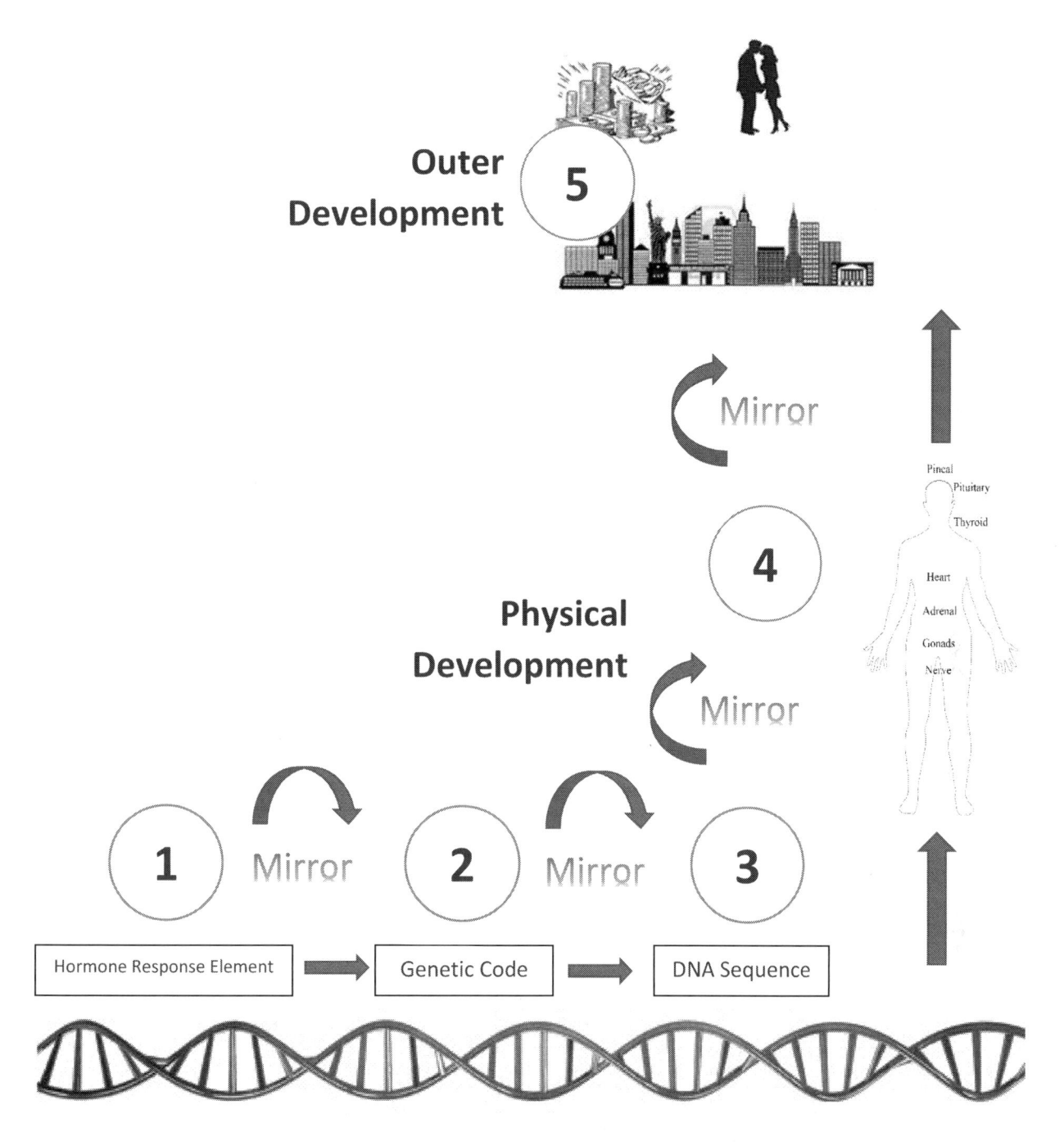

1-5 are simply expressions or mirrors of the other. Again, the point is, is that biology is not strictly tied to your body, but biology extends out to the choices you make when it comes to determining your passion and purpose, your lifestyle, and the money that you make. It is the physiological processes in the body that's designed to propel what comes to your mind when you have a determination or an intention.

Now you may wonder, what impacts the Hormone Response Element? I am glad you asked.

Your hormones are impacted by the investments coming in from others. ImbueSynthesis.
Allow me to share with you once again the following chart that documents photosynthesis alongside of ImbueSynthesis.

ImbueSynthesis

PhotoSynthesis

ImbueSynthesis

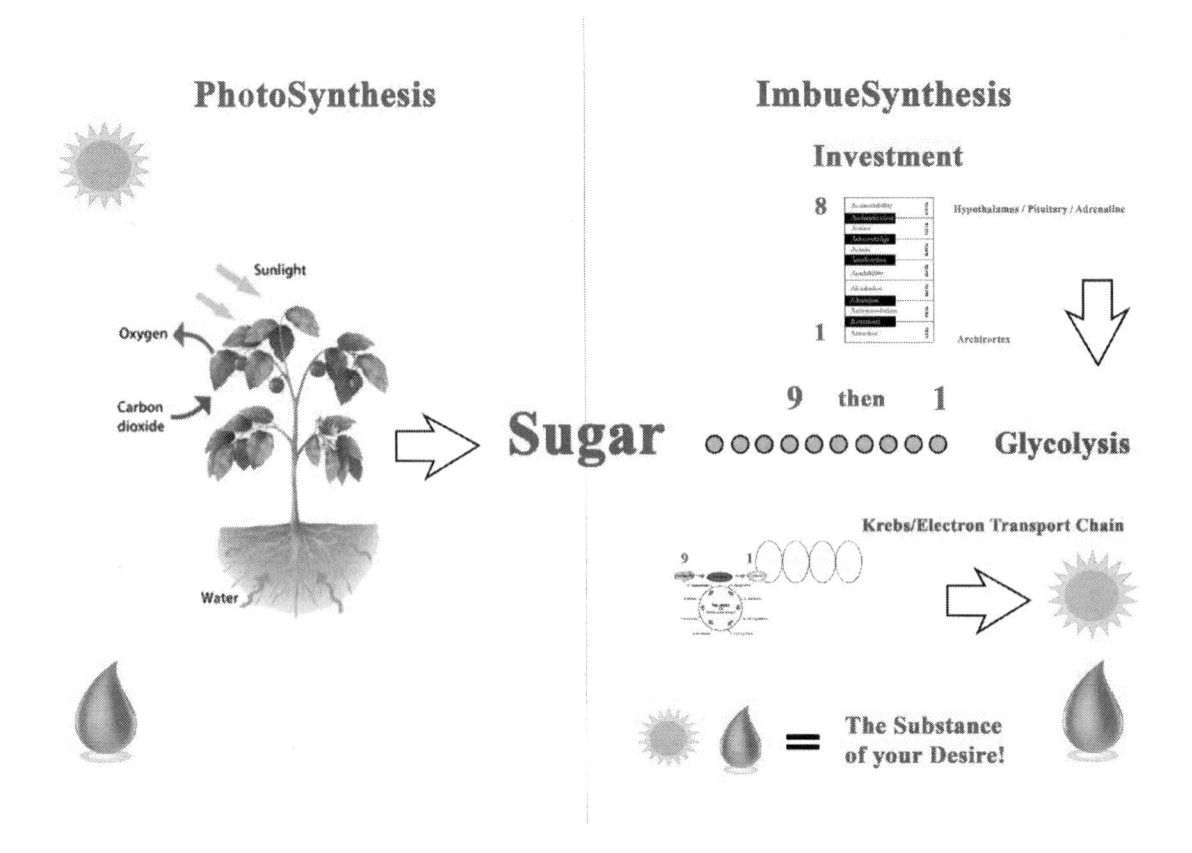

I want to remind you that ***it takes water and light to create the sugar or the memory of what a plant is***. Inverse of that, the human body produces water and light within the mitochondria of your cells. This water and light essentially becomes the stuff of your memory context or your spatial context. ***Spatial context is how you contextualize where you are going, how to get there, and what it takes to reach a state of completion.*** Imagine that, all of this extending out of mere water or converting water. Here are the investments towards you needed to make this happen.

Here are the necessary energies of investment to activate and enhance your system of memory. The energies are listed as follows:

1. Attention
2. Awareness
3. Accommodation
4. Adoration
5. Absolution
6. Availability
7. Acceleration
8. Access
9. Acknowledgement
10. Authentication (Business Relationships), Affirmation (Personal Relationships)
11. Action
12. Accountability

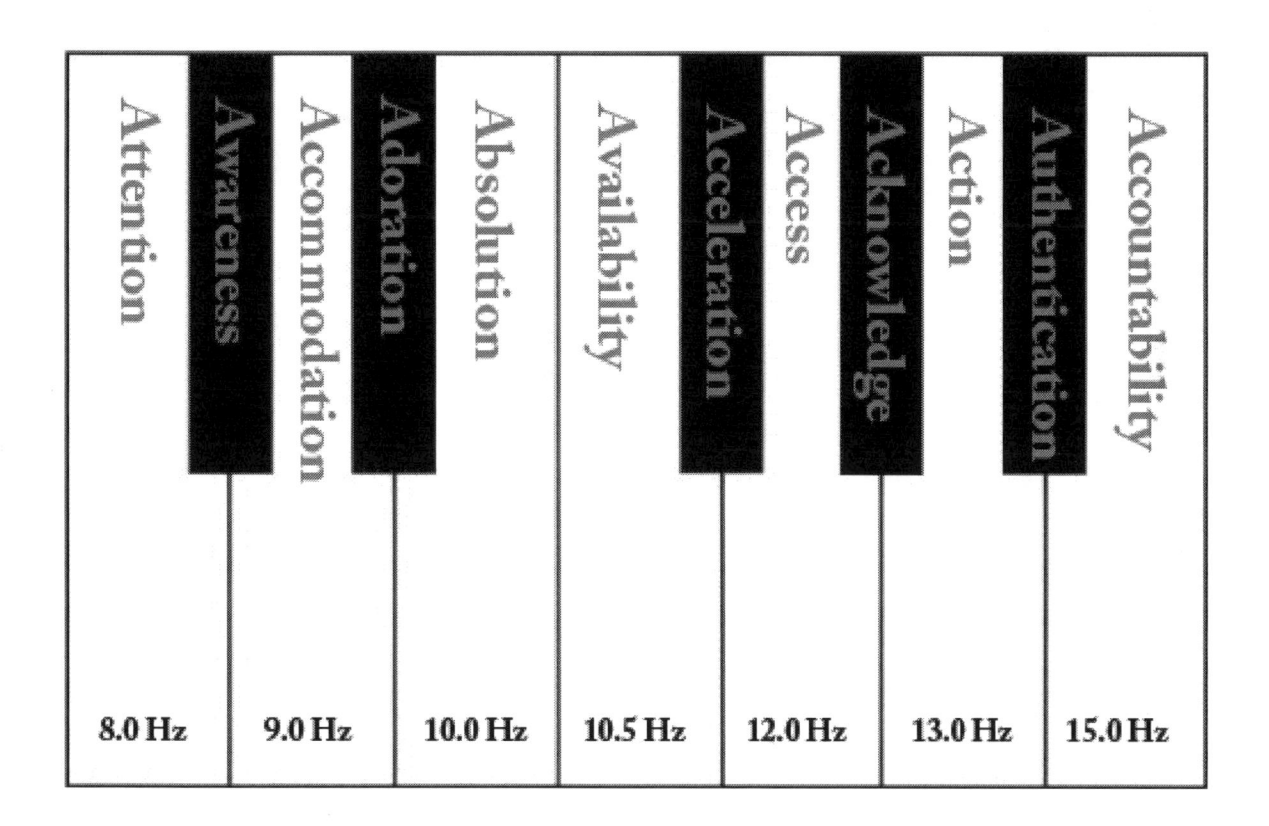

Attention	Awareness	Accommodation	Adoration	Absolution	Availability	Acceleration	Access	Acknowledge	Action	Authentication	Accountability
8.0 Hz		9.0 Hz		10.0 Hz	10.5 Hz		12.0 Hz		13.0 Hz		15.0 Hz

The way this is displayed, it is displayed on the piano scale. There is a reason for that, and that reason is because the music scale can match the energies of these same investments. I will now display the side of ImbueSynthesis for you so you can grasp the full picture. The first conversion towards any accomplishment is your exchange with another person.

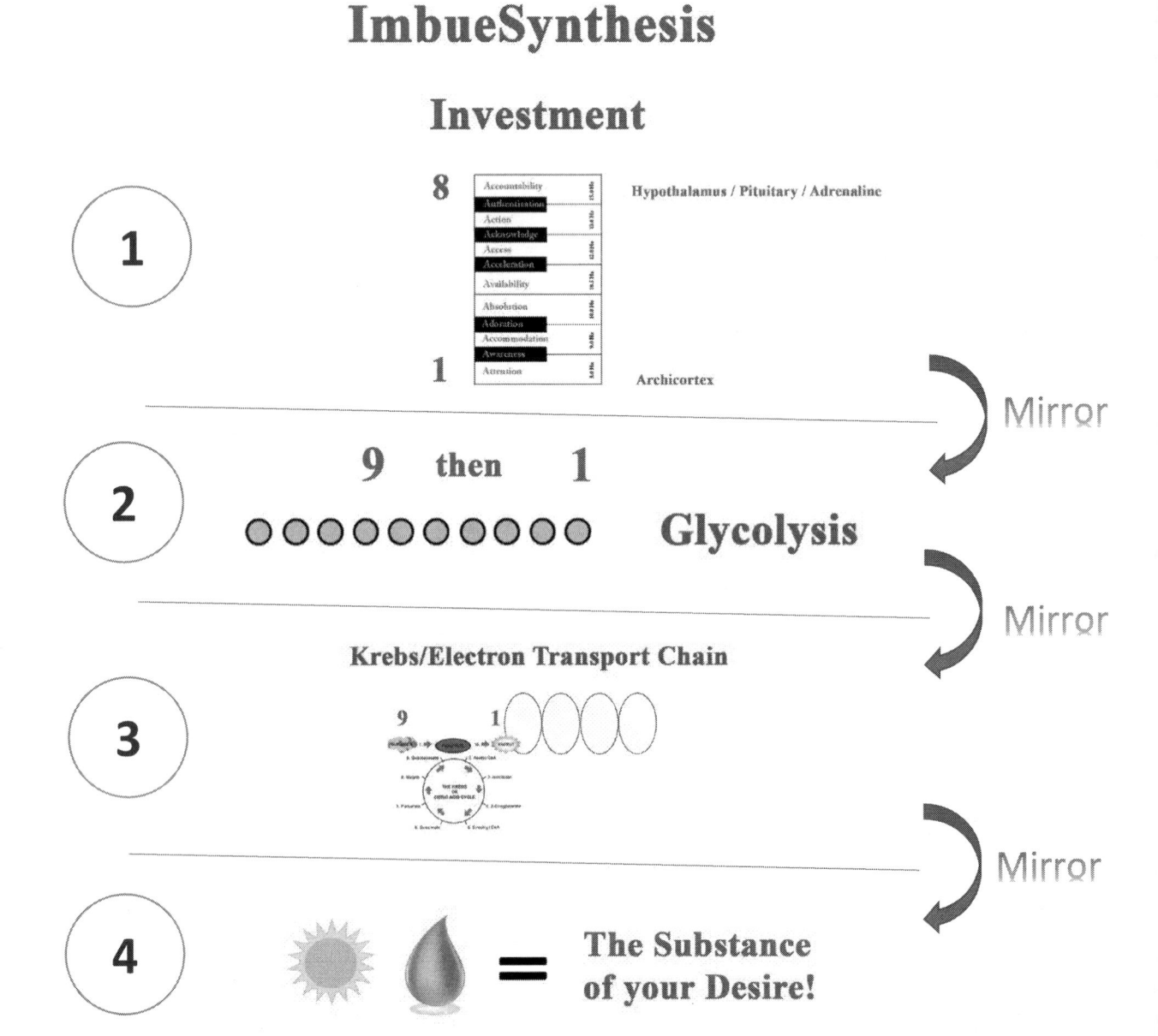

ImbueSynthesis

Investment

1

8	Accountability	Hypothalamus / Pituitary / Adrenaline
	Authentication	
	Action	
	Acknowledge	
	Access	
	Acceleration	
	Availability	
	Absorption	
	Adoration	
	Accommodation	
	Awareness	
1	Attention	Archicortex

— Mirror

2   9   then   1

○ ○ ○ ○ ○ ○ ○ ○ ○   **Glycolysis**

— Mirror

Krebs/Electron Transport Chain

3   9   1 ○○○○

— Mirror

4   ☀ 💧 =   **The Substance of your Desire!**

Don't let this seemingly confusing chart confuse you. I want you to pay strict attention to two main elements here. written in green. At the top where it says ***investment***, and at the bottom where it says ***the substance of your desires***. Then I will proceed to tell you what the stuff in the middle means.

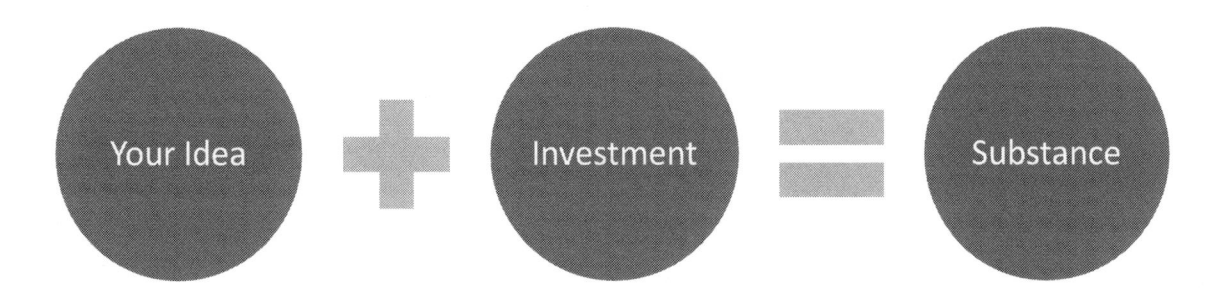

Your Idea + Investment = Substance

These 12 investments are called the Law of Agreement. And you need all 12 to sufficiently impact your cellular function. This is not a matter of exercising or dietary habits, ***it is a matter of intaking the necessary behavior patterns towards you for your body to pursue accomplishment*** from the most efficient standpoint. Here are those investments once again. You read this from the bottom up.

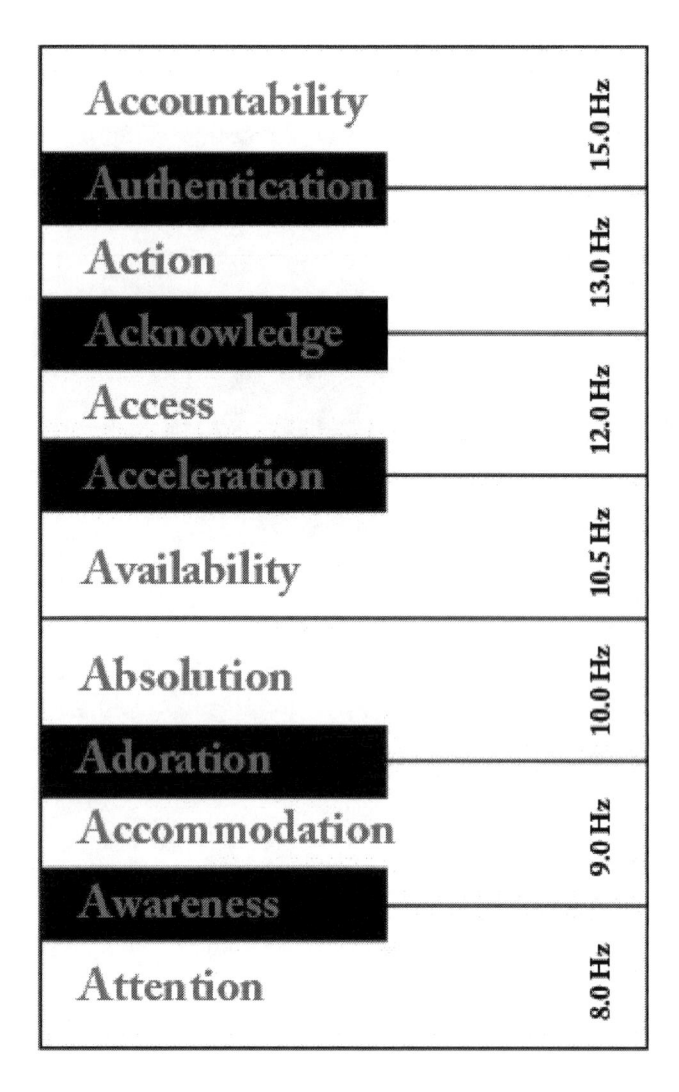

Accountability	15.0 Hz
Authentication	
Action	13.0 Hz
Acknowledge	
Access	12.0 Hz
Acceleration	
Availability	10.5 Hz
Absolution	10.0 Hz
Adoration	
Accommodation	9.0 Hz
Awareness	
Attention	8.0 Hz

I will share with you the Law of Agreement as developed by Dr. Milton Howard Jr.

The Law of Agreement

Both in personal relationships and business relationships, *Agreement is at the core of all successful relationships. Agreement is the foundation for all production and expansion, and life is not life without production and expansion that stems from Agreement*. The basis of all Universal growth and expansion is found in how you exchange, and then what extends thereafter from your exchanges. All of existence is a succession of interactions, relationships, and exchanges that advances life into continuous new existences. If you think of energy in terms of cycles, all cycles as it intertwines with other cycles produces new cycles. Effective cycles are formed from the standpoint of Agreement.

Components of "The Law of Agreement"

- Attention

- Awareness
- Accommodation
- Adoration
- Absolution
- Availability
- Acceleration
- Access
- Acknowledgement
- Authentication (Business Relationships), Affirmation (Personal Relationships)
- Action
- Accountability

Agreement is the result of these twelve energies and Agreement itself is an energy. All law is based on energy and formulations of energy, and energy is always absolute in nature. With this, **Agreement is a law that is also an energy that leads to production and expansion**. Practicing the energies or laws of Agreement will bring exacting results. The nature of all energy is law, and agreement becomes a law that lends itself to accomplishment. All energy that is properly balanced leads to absolute results.

The 1st use of "The Law of Agreement" is in your Attitude.

In Your Attitude – How You Connect

Attitude is how you project the energy of your relationship protocols and activity towards others. There must be a consciousness of the investments that you make into others. **Attitude is an "additive" energy the affects others based on the quality of practice towards others as it concerns "The Law of Agreement". This is your responsibility towards others.** Your presence is always creative within the other's existence. Your presence can also be restorative, because you "add" in value and substance based on your actions towards another. Be conscious of your ability to push others to new heights and be consistent in doing so. An "additive" is the flavor or extra energy coming from you that directly impacts the hormones and neurotransmitters of the otherperson that creates and forces new cycles within them that builds and regenerates productive energy.

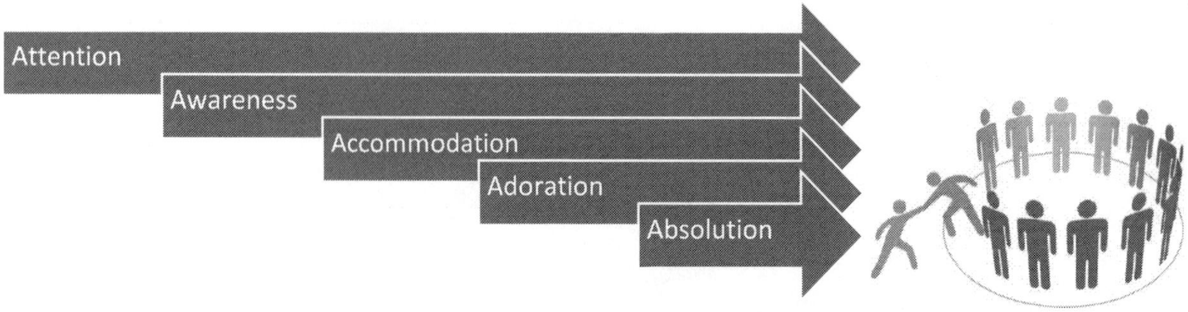
Attention
Awareness
Accommodation
Adoration
Absolution

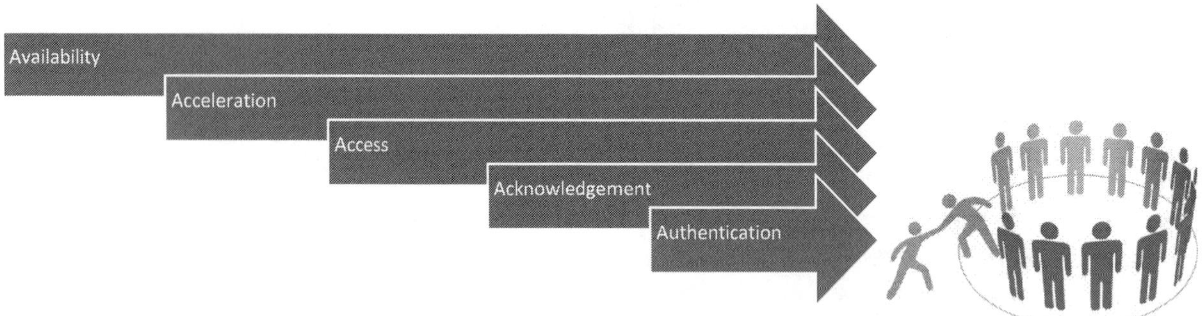
Availability
Acceleration
Access
Acknowledgement
Authentication

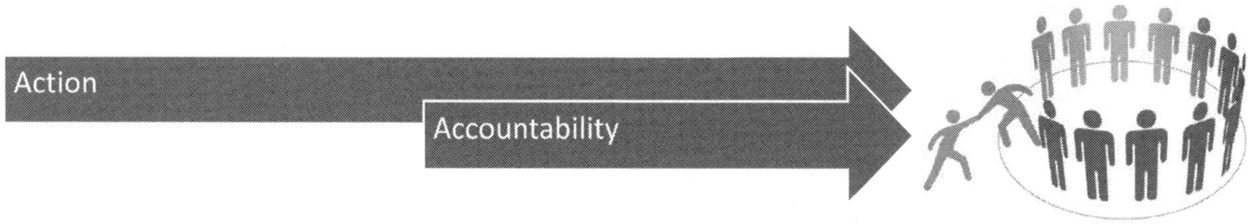
Action
Accountability

Short Statements of Agreement

Attention –

Attention is the greatest contribution of one self that can be offered. Attention received is how one knows that he or she is alive.

Awareness –

Be aware of a person's condition. Be active towards what you are aware of.

Accommodation –

Accommodation forces comfort. It is one of the most valuable parts of service.

Adoration –

Always notice what's good and be ready to speak towards that.

Absolution –

When you speak your word, follow up on your word. Integrity builds confidence in both parties. Make decisions that you can follow up on.

Availability –

Be sure to prioritize the needs of others.

Acceleration –

The role that you play in the life another should always produce results at a recognizable pace. Never be slow about producing results. Be quick to solve a problem. Answer concerns promptly.

Access –

Be inviting. Open your space. Never allow people to feel distance.

Acknowledgement –

Notice greatness. Then tell that greatness to a third party. Edify.

Authentication –

Always surround yourself with those who know more than you. Also, share your advanced knowledge to improve the life of someone else.

Action –

Always present sufficient action and present efficient action towards others that is affective and effective.

Accountability –

Hold yourself accountable in all exchanges.

The 2nd use of "The Law of Agreement" is in your Associations.

In Your Associations – How People Connect with You

All of your Associations must be measured and monitored. Associations here are the people you exchange with including your relatives, business relationships, personal, and intimate relationships. You have to take responsibility of the investments made towards you from these associations. **There must be an expectation of behavior towards yourself that is premium** in order to preserve and advance your personal well-being and wealth. People must provide you with the following qualities of agreement.

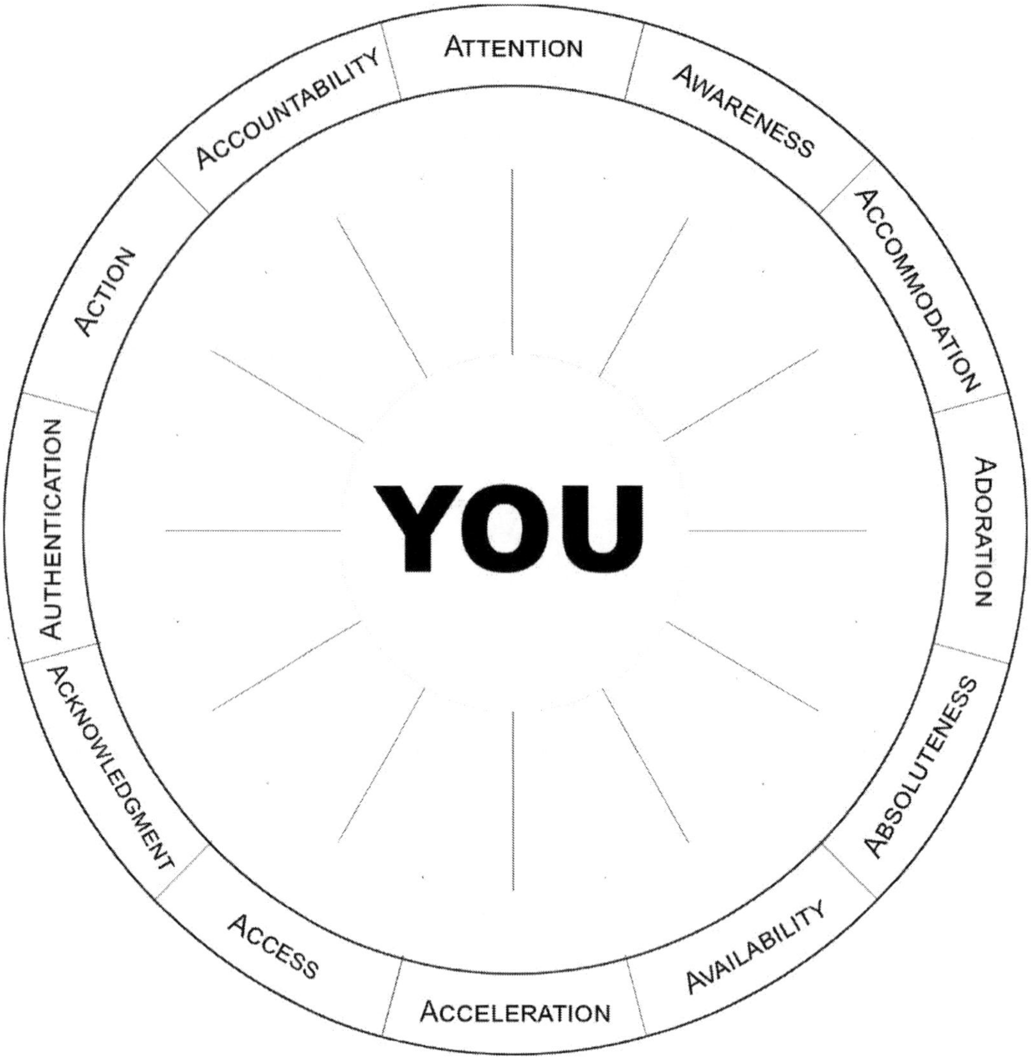
ATTENTION
AWARENESS
ACCOMMODATION
ADORATION
ABSOLUTENESS
AVAILABILITY
ACCELERATION
ACCESS
ACKNOWLEDGMENT
AUTHENTICATION
ACTION
ACCOUNTABILITY
YOU

Feelings That Stem from Agreement

Attention –

    A person feels Special.

Awareness –

    A person feels Thought of.

Accommodation –

    A person feels Comforted.

Adoration –

    A person feels Worthy.

Absolution –

    A person feels Trusting.

Availability –

    A person feels Connected.

Acceleration –

    A person feels Supported

Access –

    A person feels Accepted.

Acknowledgement –

    A person feels Promoted

Authentication –

    A person feels Exalted.

Action –

    A person feels Engaged

Accountability –

    A person feels Secure.

How a *person makes you feel* immediately impacts your personal image and translates into a reality as energy moves from the pituitary gland to the adrenal gland!

I – Mage

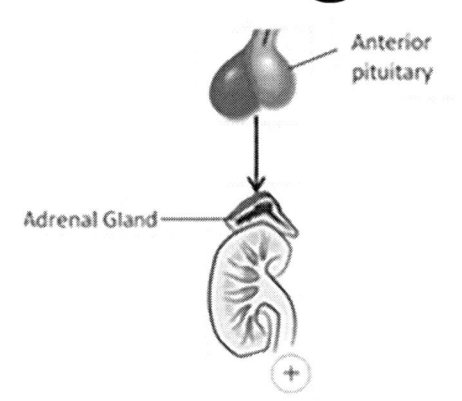

Memory

Sugar

Another use of "The Law of Agreement" is Agreement as it concerns business, entrepreneurship obtaining clients, serving clients, and valuing clients in business.

In Your Business – How You Produce Results

Instead of making sales, create agreements. Potential clients should run into a wall of energy that captivates their personal energy stemming from a genuine presentation of the Law of Agreement from you. The concentration should never be on the sell or signing up a new client, but your concentration should be focused towards the creation of a relationship stemming from Agreement and it's 12 laws or energies. This is equally true for obtaining a long-term clients or presenting an opportunity for someone make a purchase from you.

In the case of using the Law of Agreement in your business model, you can begin the Law of Agreement in a slightly different order by using these two points as the first part of obtaining an agreement:

1. **Adoration** – positive compliments as an introduction.
2. **Agreement**
    a. This is done by introducing questions that will always lead to a yes.

    After giving adoration, you can pose questions such as, "It's a beautiful day isn't it?", Yes. "You must be looking for…", Yes. "If I can help you to…would you like me to assist with…?" Yes.

3. At this time, you can move through other components in optimal order. If your using a space or display space. Invite them in. This gives a sense of **"Access"**
4. Give immediate **"Attention"** based on what you become **"Aware"** of. For example: "Let me get you some coffee…", "Let me take your coat."… Serve in some type of way.
5. **Absolution**, in offering your product or services, you must be decisive.
6. **Acceleration** – Be conscious of the pace your product or service produces results.
7. **Availability** - Beyond the point of your meeting or engagement, open yourself to being available by phone or email.
8. **Awareness** – Beyond offering to serve a client's need, hear what is being said by the client and note it, then at later points in the conversation, repeat back what you heard. This shows that you are well aware of their concerns.
9. **Acknowledgement** – If a third person is present, via **"Awareness"**, make compliments to the third party about something you noticed or heard about your potential client or customer.
10. Take **"Action"** towards something that is not a part of the sale or client acquisition, "Well in the meantime while you are considering…I'll go ahead do…for you."
11. Have some process of **"Authentication"** ready to go at all times.
12. Identify 3 or more points of future contact with your client to measure or assess satisfaction. **"Accountability"**.

By emanating these qualities of agreement, your client or customer will find themselves in your world where an exchange removes itself from being an object of question to being an object desire. If you use The Law of Agreement as it concerns your Attitude and your Associations, they will naturally reflect in your business.

Your Feelings Become Your Results

Every feeling is a hormonal state and the movement and placement of neurotransmitters in the body, and these formulating structures of state influences the physiology of the individual. Every human is genetically designed to respond to these 12 Agreements. Every component of the Law of Agreement is represented by a frequency, because every component of the Law of Agreement is energy.

The presentation of the Law of Agreement to another person activates movement of the hormones and neurotransmitters in that person's body receiving the attention. In essence, you become an artist at transforming each person you come in contact with. Be sure that you use these agreements wherein people can become artists towards you. As you are impacted by these agreements, very specific organs and body parts are immediately impacted, which in turn has a direct effect on your hormones and the hormone response element.

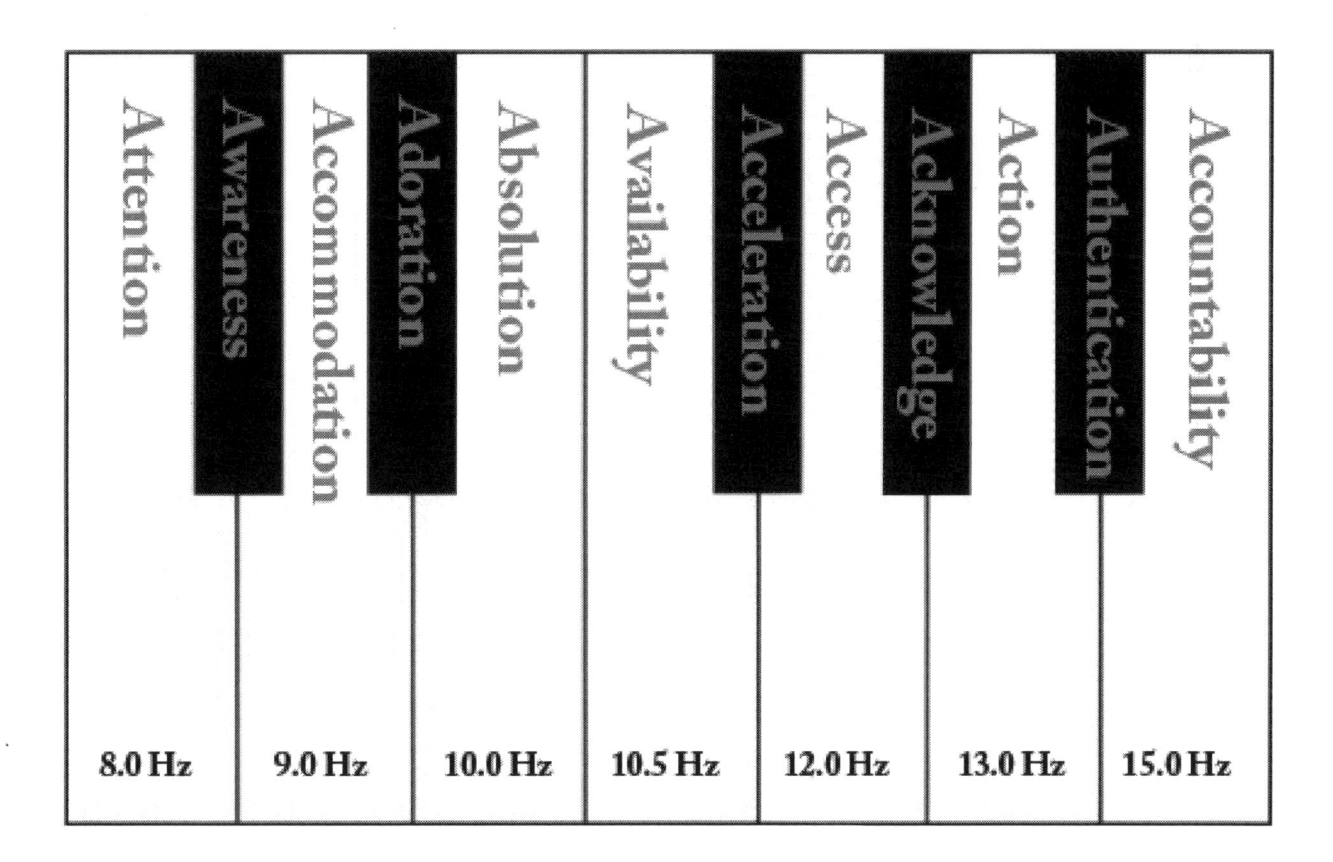

Attention	Awareness	Accommodation	Adoration	Absolution	Availability	Acceleration	Access	Acknowledge	Action	Authentication	Accountability
8.0 Hz		9.0 Hz		10.0 Hz	10.5 Hz	12.0 Hz		13.0 Hz		15.0 Hz	

8.0 Hz – Adrenal Gland, Spinal Column, Kidneys – Physical Energy, Will to Live

9.0 Hz – Reproductive Glands – Relationships

10.0 Hz – Pancreas, Serotonin, Circadian Rhythm Resync, Nervous System – Clarity, Memory

10.5 Hz – Thymus, Heart, Circulatory (Blood Pressure, Immune – Life, Love

12.0 Hz – Thyroid, Lungs, Vocal Chords – Personal Expression

13.0 Hz – Pituitary Gland, Lower Brain – Visualization

15.0 Hz – Pineal Gland, Upper Brain – Integration of Personality and Spirituality

IMPACT

Humans are genetically designed to respond to the Law of Agreement and its varied frequencies. As you display the core values of the Law of Agreement, you impact those who you come in contact with. This is ImbueSynthesis. This works equally well for personal relationships, business contacts, and sales presentations. When you creatively impact, you bring the person or audience into agreement by displaying each of the agreements within your interactions. This happens because of the physiological change that happens in the body.

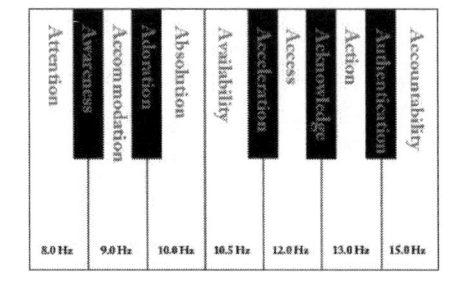

= Sugar

Sugar = Memory

It is the sugar that converts into water and memory, which then becomes the substance of who you are, and more importantly, who you will become.

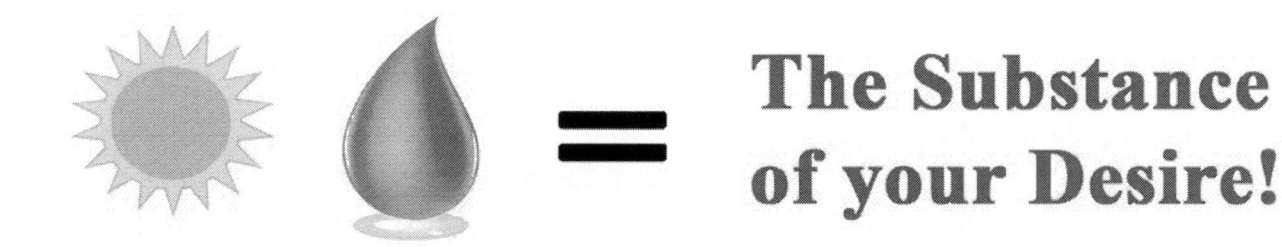

= The Substance of your Desire!

To get to the water and light into your cells, you have a process called Glycolysis. Once again, this is for the purpose of the professional who is reading this text. But when you grasp a strong sense of the total process and can manage the stages of conversions that's naturally taking place, you will be more enabled to master the conversions outside of yourself that lead to your personal accomplishments. I can't really leave anything out. With this, when you can get a solid grasp on your purpose and passion, your lifestyle, and your money, **when one expresses the 12 Agreements towards you, it more acutely impacts the activation of glycolysis in your cells**. Essentially taking sugar and creating water and light.

Pay attention to the 10 steps of Glycolysis. It converts 9 times before it produces its final stage. Once again, this is the expertise built within your body that is a mastery of conversion.

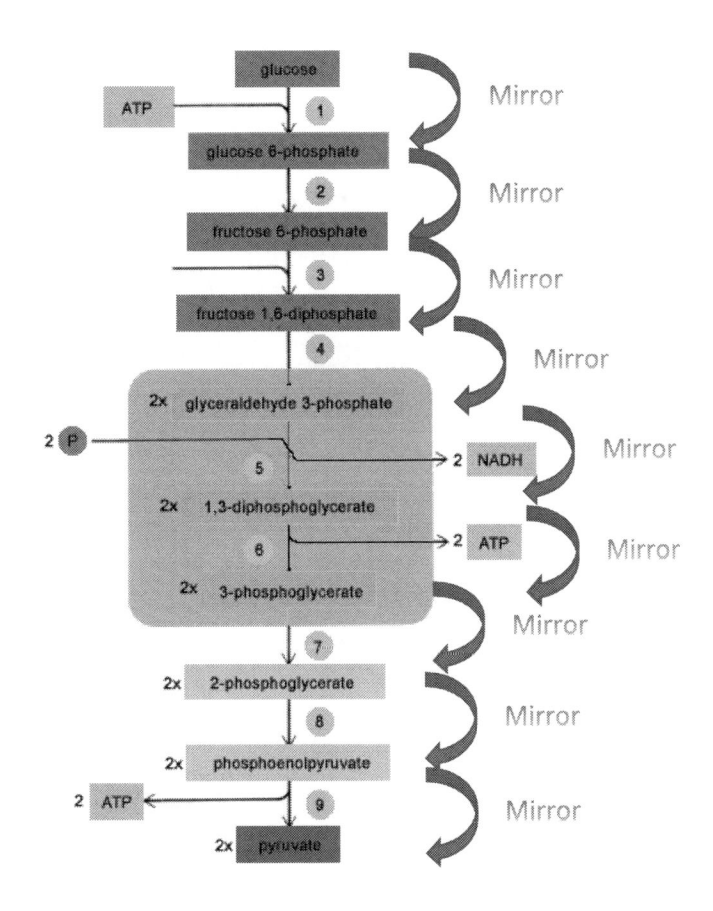

Every part of your body practices conversion as it mirrors a previous existence. This sets the stage for you to convert what's in your mind into reality. You do millions of times a day. You are an expert!

1. How You See Things (Perception)
2. Your Every Action (Exception and Exceptional)
3. The Law of Agreement Invested Into You

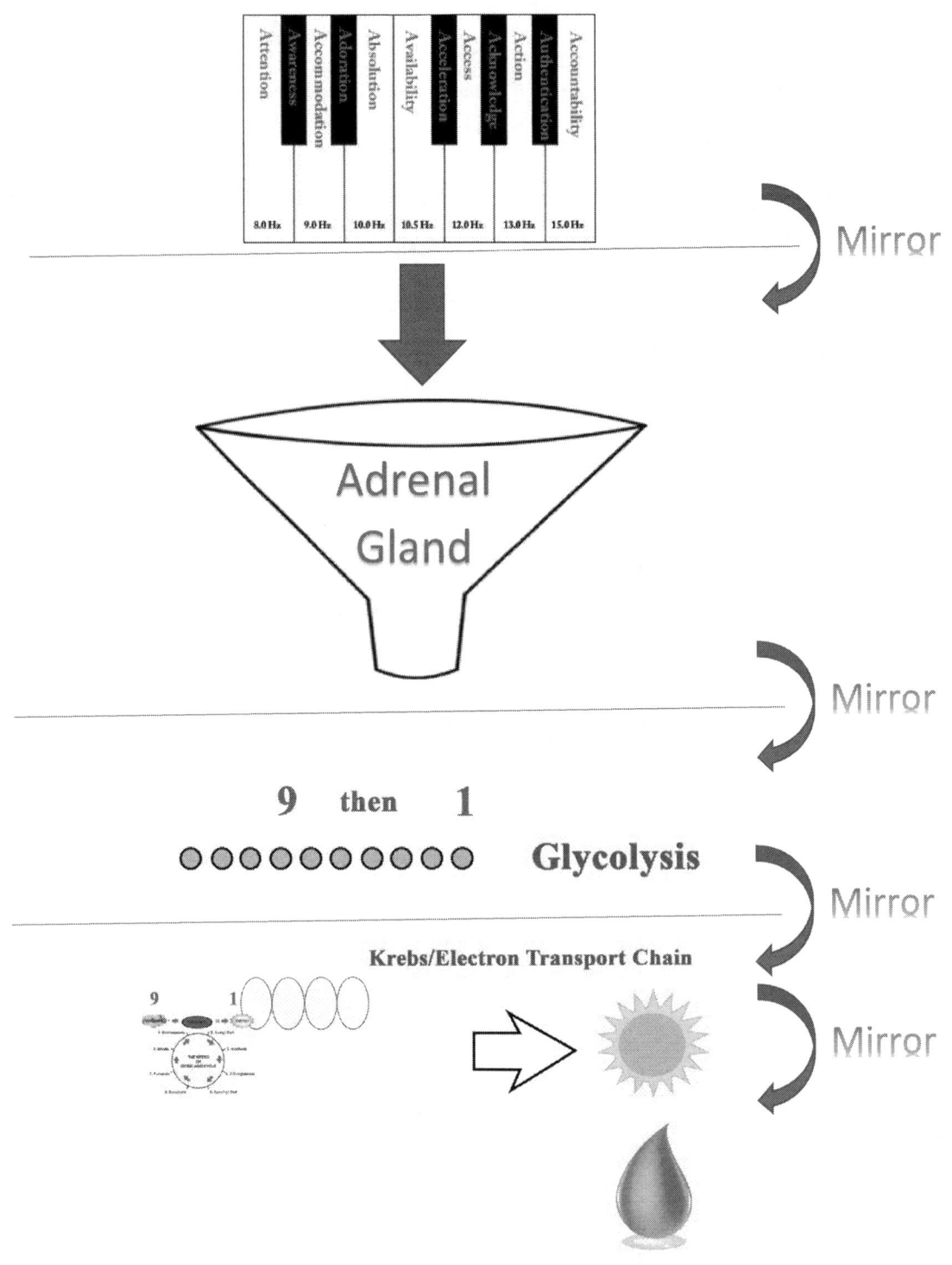

The end result is water and light when you are properly agreed with and the personages around you can actively portray the necessary investments into your passion, purpose, and your designed destiny.
So, what is this? Every scientific and biological process in your body contributes to your end game.

9 then 1

○○○○○○○○○ Glycolysis = **Energy**

Krebs/Electron Transport Chain

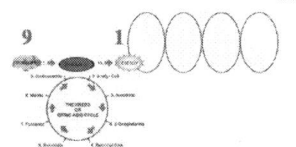

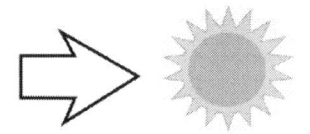

= **What You Want**

1. Glycolysis
   a. 9 then 1 refers to the 9 stages of sugar transforming in your cells to create energy, the 10th stage or the 1 is the final stage.
   b. This is activated when the adrenaline from your adrenal gland is released.
   c. Impacted by how one treats you and invests in you.
2. Krebs Cycle
   a. The Kreb Cycle or Citric Acid Cycle takes the results of Glycolysis and further develops the energy in 10 stages also.
   b. This result is deposited into the Electron Transport Chain.
3. The Electron Transport Chain
   a. The ETC are four chambers in which the energy molecule travels.
   b. With hydrogen atoms being released into the cell during this process, water and energy molecules are deposited into the cell for your personal use.

The point is this, your body in multiple stages is practicing success, leaving you with the "stuff" to accomplish whatever you want in life. This whole process is first activated by the quality of investments you are receiving from others. Needless to say, **the quality of investments that you receive in life impacts how you remember your future**. Memory of the past is a given. Building memory for the future is a gift of potential and potency and must be managed by managing how people treat you.

What I'm displaying here is the fact that you are physiologically impacted by the attention that you get, and a person's awareness of you, whether or not someone is accommodating, the words that people speak towards you, people keeping their word, people making themselves available to you, and so on.

This immediately determines how your cholesterol behaves and how it is processed in the adrenal gland. It determines the release of adrenaline into your bloodstream and its impact on your cells. It takes this "impact" and translates it through glycolysis to create energy. Then in the end, water and light. All of this is contributing to what you want and towards the energy to obtain it.

Outer Development

1 Investment

6

Physical Development

5

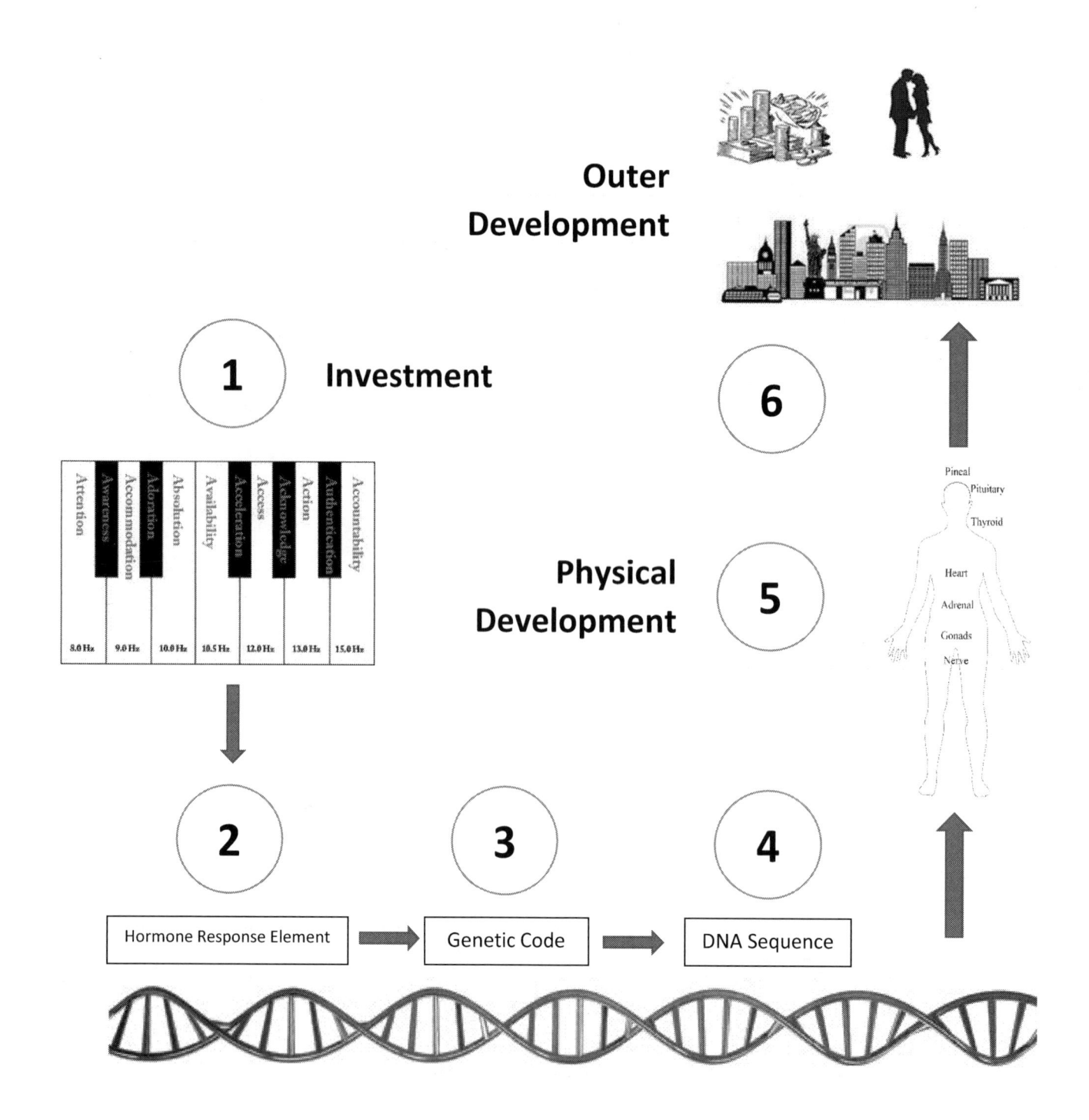

2 → Hormone Response Element → **3** Genetic Code → **4** DNA Sequence

Let's make sure this happens by documenting who's investing and who is not. This is absolutely necessary, as you have to be completely responsible for who's making the right moves in your life. You must also take the time to mark whose life you are investing these same qualities into. The best way to be aware of these qualities coming towards you is to practice sharing these same qualities with others.

HPA Axis

Relax

1 ← **I – Mage**

Your I – Mage Starts here…

Your connections must

2 ← **Agree**

This is your Evolutionary Equal. *Mirror*

Only then does

3 ← **Memory**

formulate correctly… *Mirror*

Your Destiny is

4 ← **Imminent**

at this point. *Mirror*

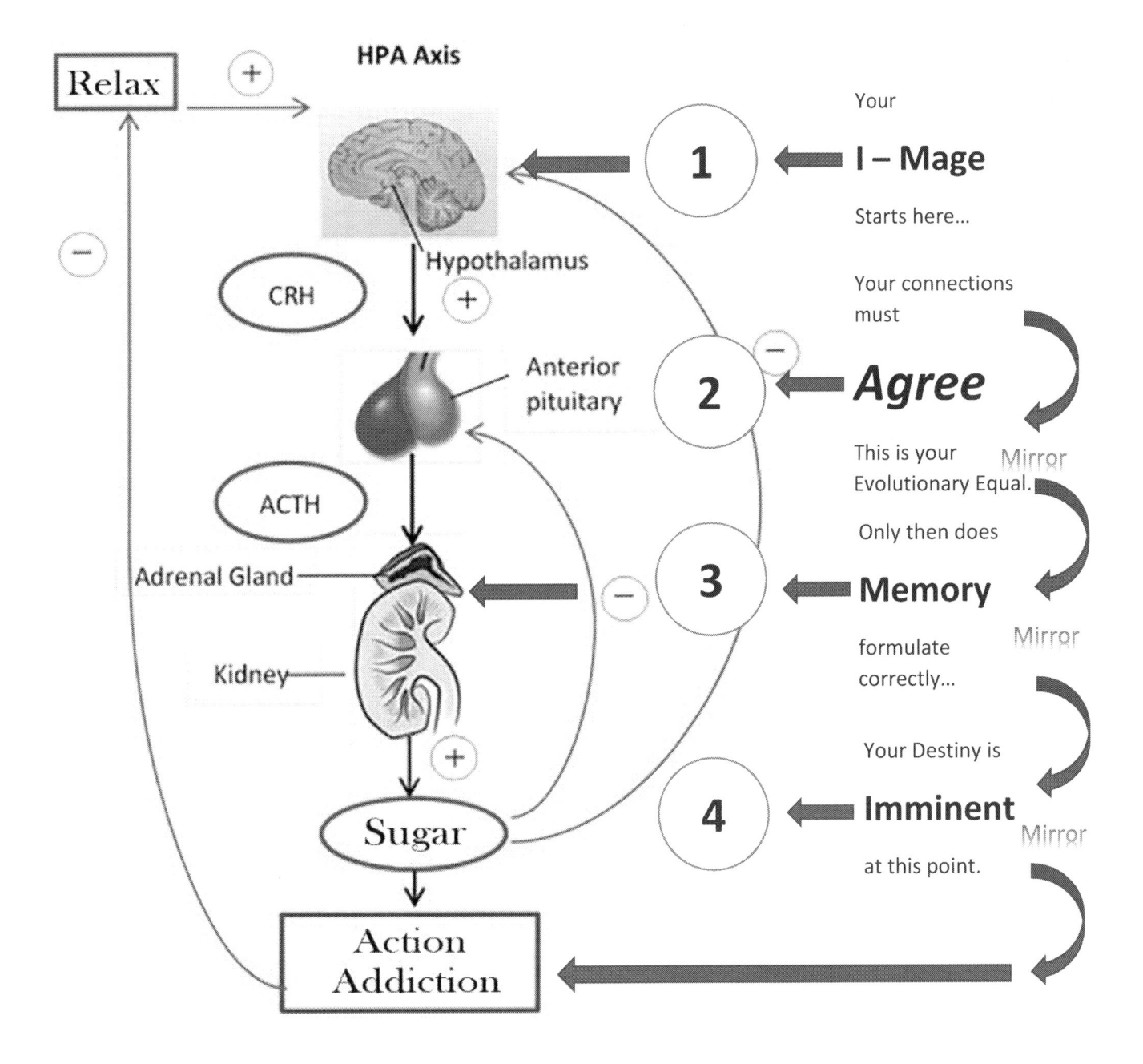

Action Addiction

At this point, I would like to be extremely clear. It is almost exclusively step 2 where most people fail because this is an area of diminished focus. Correct relationships are vital towards accomplishment.

Success is a matter of biology!

Success is not a matter of planning, strategy, birthright, education, long hours, and the like. Success is a matter of science and relationships are a science and you must treat it as such. Pay attention to your diminished capacity when you're with the wrong person or the wrong people. When those that you associate with does not have the capacity or capability to invest in you according to where you want to go and what you want, you will lose. The loss is scientific. Document those who agree in the following.

- Attention

1. Who's Investing   Who's Not
   _____   _____
   _____   _____
   _____   _____
   _____   _____
   _____   _____

- Awareness

2. Who's Investing   Who's Not
   _____   _____
   _____   _____
   _____   _____
   _____   _____
   _____   _____

- Accommodation

3. Who's Investing   Who's Not
   _____   _____
   _____   _____
   _____   _____
   _____   _____
   _____   _____

- Adoration

4. Who's Investing   Who's Not

   _____   _____
   _____   _____
   _____   _____
   _____   _____
   _____   _____

- Absolution

    5. Who's Investing   Who's Not

       _____   _____
       _____   _____
       _____   _____
       _____   _____
       _____   _____

- Availability

    6. Who's Investing   Who's Not

       _____   _____
       _____   _____
       _____   _____
       _____   _____
       _____   _____

- Acceleration

7. Who's Investing   Who's Not

   _____   _____
   _____   _____
   _____   _____
   _____   _____
   _____   _____

- Access

8. Who's Investing   Who's Not

   _____   _____
   _____   _____
   _____   _____
   _____   _____
   _____   _____

- Acknowledgement

9. Who's Investing   Who's Not

   _____   _____
   _____   _____
   _____   _____
   _____   _____
   _____   _____

- Authentication (Business Relationships), Affirmation (Personal Relationships)

10. Who's Investing   Who's Not

_____   _____

_____   _____

_____   _____

_____   _____

_____   _____

- Action

11. Who's Investing   Who's Not

_____   _____

_____   _____

_____   _____

_____   _____

_____   _____

- Accountability

12. Who's Investing   Who's Not

_____   _____

_____   _____

_____   _____

_____   _____

_____   _____

Now list the people who you plan to invest these specific agreements into. In an effort of responsibility, please date the time you intend to serve. Pay attention to the depth of your investment.

- Attention

1. Who   What date?

   _____   _____
   _____   _____
   _____   _____
   _____   _____
   _____   _____

- Awareness

2. Who   What date?

   _____   _____
   _____   _____
   _____   _____
   _____   _____
   _____   _____

- Accommodation

3. Who   What date?

   _____   _____
   _____   _____
   _____   _____
   _____   _____
   _____   _____

- Adoration

4. Who   What date?

_____   _____

_____   _____

_____   _____

_____   _____

_____   _____

- Absolution

5. Who   What date?

_____   _____

_____   _____

_____   _____

_____   _____

_____   _____

- Availability

6. Who   What date?

_____   _____

_____   _____

_____   _____

_____   _____

_____   _____

- Acceleration

7. Who   What date?
   _____   _____
   _____   _____
   _____   _____
   _____   _____
   _____   _____

- Access

8. Who   What date?
   _____   _____
   _____   _____
   _____   _____
   _____   _____
   _____   _____

- Acknowledgement

9. Who   What date?
   _____   _____
   _____   _____
   _____   _____
   _____   _____
   _____   _____

- Authentication (Business Relationships), Affirmation (Personal Relationships)

10. Who   What date?

   _____   _____
   _____   _____
   _____   _____
   _____   _____
   _____   _____

- Action

11. Who   What date?

   _____   _____
   _____   _____
   _____   _____
   _____   _____
   _____   _____

- Accountability

12. Who   What date?

   _____   _____
   _____   _____
   _____   _____
   _____   _____
   _____   _____

The 12 Points of Significance

The 12 Points of Significance is a series of investments coming from others into you. Just like the Law of Agreement, you must expect these investments. You are the manager of these investments. You must be aware of what you don't have when it comes to investments. These investments activate a completeness in you, which in turn impacts your passion and purpose. Here they are:

Wheel diagram with "YOU" at the center, surrounded by 12 points:
- VIEWED
- UNDERSTOOD
- ENGAGED
- PRAISED
- BELIEVED
- PRIORITIZED
- ENRICHED
- ADVANCED
- REWARDED
- EXALTED
- INCREASED
- DOUBLED

1
(To Be Viewed)

The Investment of seeing and knowing a person.
Everyone needs someone to see and know who they are.

2
(To Be Comprehended)
The Investment of understanding a person.
Everyone has a need to be understood.

3
(To Be Engaged)
The Investment of active commitment.
Everyone has a need to be touched in some way.

4
(To Be Praised)
The Investment of vocal affirmation of the good.
Everyone has a need to hear something good about themselves.

5
(To Be Believed)
The Investment of trust.
Everyone has a need to be trusted and believed in.

6
(To Be Prioritized)
The Investment of making one special.
Everyone has the need to feel number one sometimes.

7
(To Be Enrihed)
The Investment of provision.
Everyone has a need to receive.

8
(To Be Advanced)
The Investment of pushing one forward.

Everyone has a need to be mentored or pushed forward.

9
(To Be Rewarded)
The Investment of recognition.
Everyone has a need to be appreciated in a tangible way.

10
(To Be Exalted)
The Investment of one's self into another.
Everyone has a need to feel another's presence that builds their own presence.

11
(To Be Increased)
The Investment of addition.
Everyone has a need to be completed by the investment of another's effort and partnership.

12
(To Be Doubled)
The Investment of multiplication.
Everyone has a need to grow by the investment of another's effort or partnership.

Now I will expand upon the idea of each investment. Study them, because you have to begin to measure or take measurement of these presences in your life.

1
(To Be Viewed)
The Investment of seeing and knowing a person.

- To know a person as in their habits, favorite things, concerns etc.

- To be concerned and having a person's back based on what you see in them.

- See, recognize, and care for one's issues.

Everyone needs someone to see and know who they are.

2
(To Be Comprehended)
The Investment of understanding a person.

- Understanding of one's issues.

- Willing to take in right information concerning a person.

- Agreement and right action towards that understanding of the person.

Everyone has a need to be understood.

3
(To Be Engaged)
The Investment of active commitment.

- Physical connection.

- Partnership and unification.

- Two way exchange or communication.

Everyone has a need to be touched in some way.

4
(To Be Praised)
The Investment of vocal affirmation of the good.

- Recognition and hearing about good attributes.

- Complimentary in nature towards a person.

- Approvals of ideas, thoughts, visions...etc.

Everyone has a need to hear something good about themselves.

5
(To Be Believed)
The Investment of trust.

- Take a position based on concerns verbalized, or character exuded.

- Action oriented belief qualified by action oriented support.

- Taking responsibility and acting on a person's behalf based believing in them.

Everyone has a need to be trusted and believed in.

6
(To Be Prioritized)
The Investment of making one special.

- Acute attention in certain situations and areas.

- Putting things aside in recognition of the other.

- Allowing a person from time to time to be the most important.

Everyone has the need to feel number one sometimes.

7
(To Be Enriched)
The Investment of provision.

- Bringing gifts or supplies not associated with earning.

- Sharing your personal substance.

- Making sure a person's needs are met.

Everyone has a need to receive.

8
(To Be Advanced)
The Investment of pushing one forward.

- Progressing one's effort by means of time and efforts.

- Providing leadership in your area of expertise to advance the cause of another.

- To give an effort in setting a situation or circumstance right.

Everyone has a need to be mentored or pushed forward.

9
(To Be Rewarded)
The Investment of recognition.

- To provide substance in recognition of what someone has invested in you.

- Physical substance given in appreciation for efforts made.

- Thank you and appreciation outside of verbal affirmation.

Everyone has a need to be appreciated in a tangible way.

10
(To Be Exalted)
The Investment of one's self into another.

- Time spent in all areas of emotional investments.

- Giving a sense of place based on your presence.

- The gift of yourself that lift a person to another level, give status or empowers.

Everyone has a need to feel another's presence that builds their own presence.

11
(To Be Increased)
The Investment of addition.

- To empower, enhance or enable in any way.

- To see then add in a positive way time, effort, or substance.

- To be an extension for someone where someone comes short.

Everyone has a need to be completed by the investment of another's effort and partnership.

12
(To Be Doubled)
The Investment of multiplication.

- The experience of results.

- Results that lead to more results.

- Results that give a sense of place, home, completeness.

Everyone has a need to grow by the investment of another's effort or partnership.

As you can see; your relationships and how they are set up, play a vital role in your ability to see and experience your life at its best. This is the true beginning of everything economic. Remember, energy is personal psychological money. In order to live a fuller and more exciting life, you must prepare yourself to receive your full supply of what's for you by setting your perception and aligning your relationships in order to keep focused on your own good and producing good.

Step 1

Start documenting the persons who fit into these 12 slots. Remember your words and language is important to your personal development. With this being the case, you want to enable yourself to have quality conversations. These 12 types of relative energy dynamics will provide the basis for empowering conversations.

1
(To Be Viewed)
Who sees who you are and respects that?
The Investment of seeing and knowing a person.

_____
_____
_____
_____

Everyone needs someone to see and know who they are.

2
(To Be Comprehended)
Who understands you? Who understands your ideas and language?
The Investment of understanding a person.

_____
_____
_____
_____

Everyone has a need to be understood.

3
(To Be Engaged)
Who gets actively involved in what you are doing?
The Investment of active commitment.

_____
_____

_____
_____

Everyone has a need to be touched in some way.

4
(To Be Praised)
Who pays you kind words? Who are the people who can see and say the good?
The Investment of vocal affirmation of the good.

_____
_____
_____
_____

Everyone has a need to hear something good about themselves.

5
(To Be Believed)
Who trusts you because of you? Who rapidly responds to you based on trust?
The Investment of trust.

_____
_____
_____
_____

Everyone has a need to be trusted and believed in.

6
(To Be Prioritized)
Who takes the time from time to time to put you first?
The Investment of making one special.

_____
_____
_____

_____

Everyone has the need to feel number one sometimes.

7
(To Be Enriched)
Who gives to you just because?
The Investment of provision.

_____
_____
_____
_____

Everyone has a need to receive.

8
(To Be Advanced)
Who pushes you to the next level?
The Investment of pushing one forward.

_____
_____
_____
_____

Everyone has a need to be mentored or pushed forward.

9
(To Be Rewarded)
Who sees your contributions and acts towards it through recognizing you in a tangible way?
The Investment of recognition.

_____
_____
_____

_____

Everyone has a need to be appreciated in a tangible way.

10
(To Be Exalted)
Who gives you their support, but not just in words or verbal sentiment? Who shows up?
The Investment of one's self into another.

_____
_____
_____
_____

Everyone has a need to feel another's presence that builds their own presence.

11
(To Be Increased)
Who gives you their time and talent in areas that you are not the best in?
The Investment of addition.

_____
_____
_____
_____

Everyone has a need to be completed by the investment of another's effort and partnership.

12
(To Be Doubled)
Who agrees with you and is willing to act towards that agreement?
The Investment of multiplication.

_____
_____
_____
_____

Everyone has a need to grow by the investment of another's effort or partnership.

1. How You See Things (Perception)
2. Your Every Action (Exception and Exceptional)
3. The Law of Agreement (Conception)
4. 12 Points of Significance

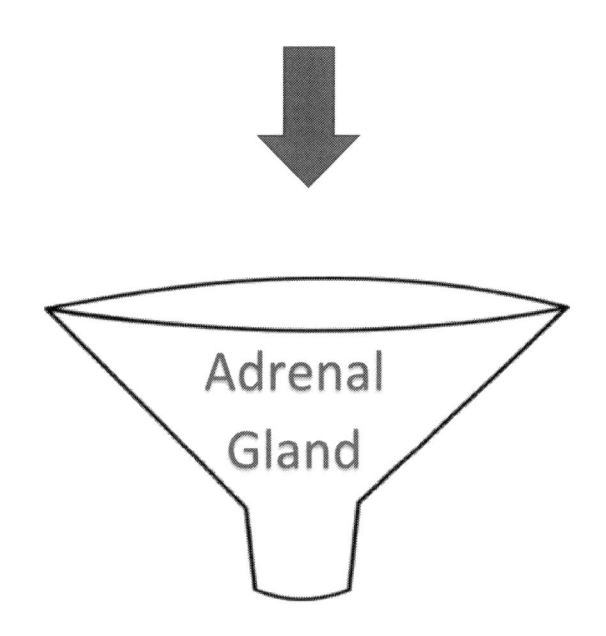

⬇

Adrenal Gland

Step 2

Make sure you enact these same points of significance towards others.

1
(View Someone)
**The Investment of seeing and knowing a person.
Everyone needs someone to see and know who they are.**

2
(Comprehended Someone)
The Investment of understanding a person.
Everyone has a need to be understood.

3
(Engage Someone)
The Investment of active commitment.
Everyone has a need to be touched in some way.

4
(Give Someone Praise)
The Investment of vocal affirmation of the good.
Everyone has a need to hear something good about themselves.

5
(Believe in Someone)
The Investment of trust.
Everyone has a need to be trusted and believed in.

6
(Prioritize Someone)
The Investment of making one special.
Everyone has the need to feel number one sometimes.

7
(Enrich Someone's Life)
The Investment of provision.
Everyone has a need to receive.

8
(Advance Someone)
The Investment of pushing one forward.
Everyone has a need to be mentored or pushed forward.

9
(Reward Someone)
The Investment of recognition.
Everyone has a need to be appreciated in a tangible way.

10
(Exalt Someone)
The Investment of one's self into another.
Everyone has a need to feel another's presence that builds their own presence.

11
(Increase Someone)
The Investment of addition.
Everyone has a need to be completed by the investment of another's effort and partnership.

12
(Be Someone's Double)
The Investment of multiplication.
Everyone has a need to grow by the investment of another's effort or partnership.

This gives the totality of your energy its balance. That's why it is vital to document and measure these 12 points. Relationships become a vital part of self-recognition. It is within the self that all knowledge is contained. Without the right people around you, it becomes difficult to draw on this knowledge. Many people spend thousands of dollars to institutions and individuals seeking higher knowledge, but all knowledge is contained within. You can serve as your own model.

Now use the same 12 Points to determine how you will serve others.

- Who needs to be seen?

1. Who   What date?

   _____   _____
   _____   _____
   _____   _____
   _____   _____
   _____   _____

- Who needs to be understood?

2. Who   What date?

   _____   _____
   _____   _____
   _____   _____
   _____   _____
   _____   _____

- Who needs to be engaged?

3. Who   What date?

   _____   _____
   _____   _____
   _____   _____
   _____   _____
   _____   _____

- Who needs to be praised?

4. Who   What date?

   _____   _____
   _____   _____
   _____   _____
   _____   _____
   _____   _____

- Who needs to be believed?

   5. Who   What date?

   _____   _____
   _____   _____
   _____   _____
   _____   _____
   _____   _____

- Who needs to be prioritized?

   6. Who   What date?

   _____   _____
   _____   _____
   _____   _____
   _____   _____
   _____   _____

- Who needs to be enriched?

7. Who   What date?

  _____ _____
  _____ _____
  _____ _____
  _____ _____
  _____ _____

- Who needs to be advanced?

8. Who   What date?

  _____ _____
  _____ _____
  _____ _____
  _____ _____
  _____ _____

- Who needs to be rewarded?

9. Who   What date?

  _____ _____
  _____ _____
  _____ _____
  _____ _____
  _____ _____

- Who needs to be exalted?

10. Who   What date?
   _____   _____
   _____   _____
   _____   _____
   _____   _____
   _____   _____

- Who needs to be increased?

11. Who   What date?
   _____   _____
   _____   _____
   _____   _____
   _____   _____
   _____   _____

- Who needs to be mirrored?

12. Who   What date?
   _____   _____
   _____   _____
   _____   _____
   _____   _____
   _____   _____

Outer ring (clockwise from top): Viewed, Understood, Engaged, Praised, Believed, Prioritized, Enriched, Advanced, Rewarded, Exalted, Increased, Doubled

Inner ring (clockwise from top): Attention, Awareness, Accommodation, Adoration, Absoluteness, Availability, Acceleration, Access, Acknowledgment, Authentication, Action, Accountability

Center: **YOU**

⬇

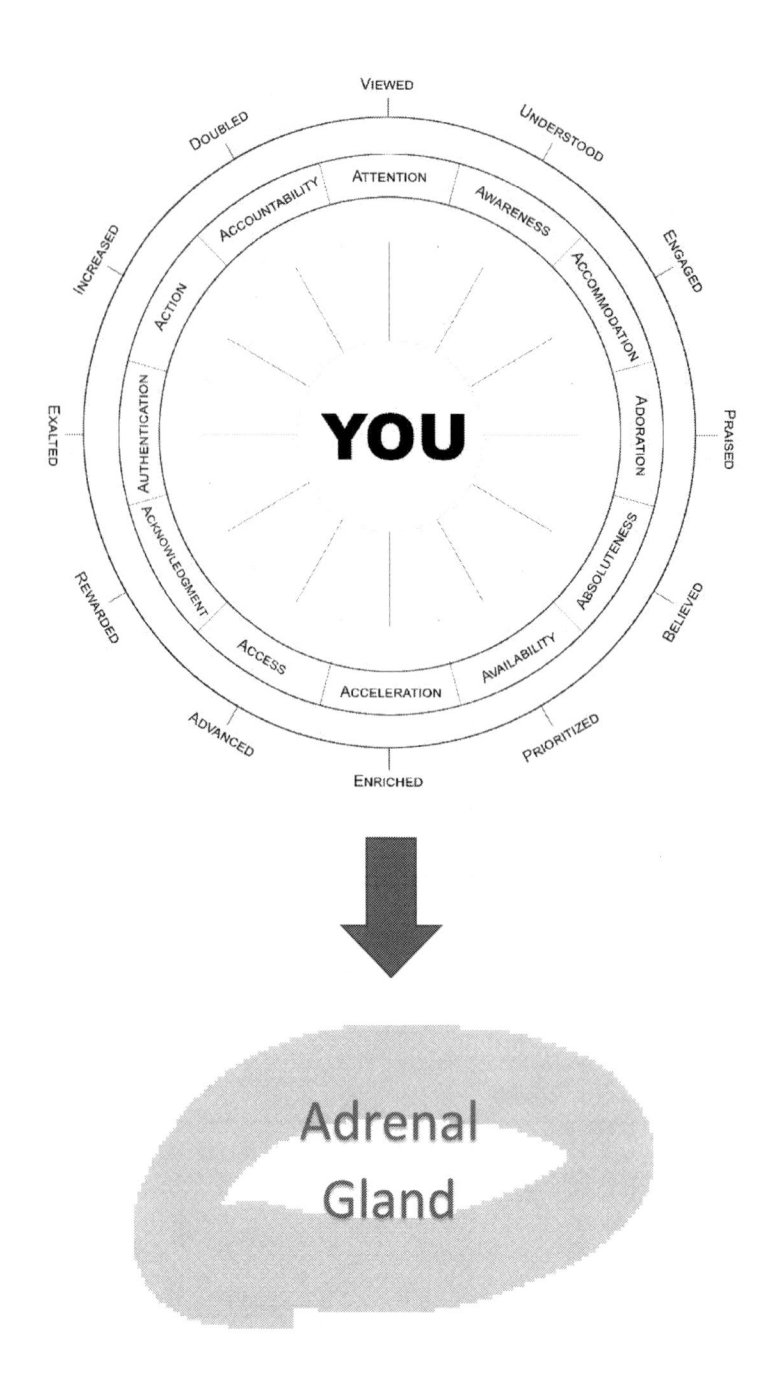

Adrenal Gland

Becomes

What & How

You Remember

SUGAR

SUGAR = Memory

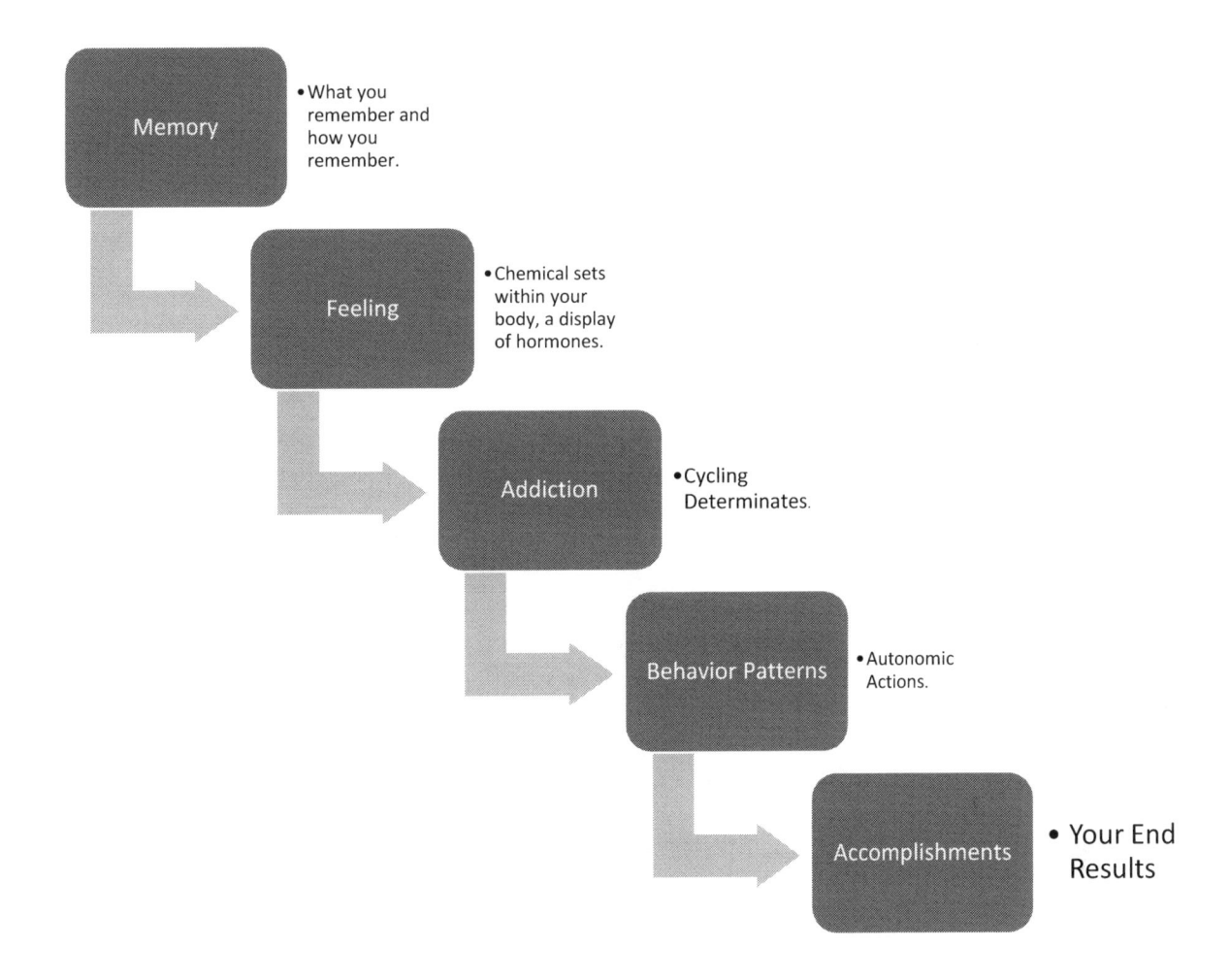

- **Memory** — What you remember and how you remember.
- **Feeling** — Chemical sets within your body, a display of hormones.
- **Addiction** — Cycling Determinates.
- **Behavior Patterns** — Autonomic Actions.
- **Accomplishments** — Your End Results

Essentially, when it comes to accomplishments, you must become clear about what you want. You now have the tools for clarity. Once, clarity is set, do not create another reality through the denial of your own greatness. Do not tell yourself stories or even lie to yourself in an effort to change directions.

Use this workbook. Do the work. The most important pathway towards accomplishment is the structure of your relationships. 90% of issues that present themselves as blockages towards your intentions rest in your relationships. So, they must be managed

Now you must take the necessary actions to accomplish your desires. Start. Go. Move forward.

Made in United States
Orlando, FL
06 February 2024